PRAISE FOR *THE LINE MAKER*

"If you liked Patrick Lencioni's *The Five Dysfunctions of a Team* and Mitch Albom's *The Five People You Meet in Heaven*, you are going to LOVE this book!"

— **Davin Salvagno**, Bestselling Author of *Thieves of Purpose* and *Finding Purpose at Work*

"*The Line Maker* is an instant classic! Powerful principles combined with a compelling story create space for the reader to experience true transformation. In the spirit of a great Og Mandino tale, *The Line Maker* will be read, reread, studied, and passed along for decades to come. This is inspired and inspiring!"

— **Boyd C. Matheson**, Former Radio/TV Host and International Business Strategist

"As a professional artist with over thirty years of experience, I've learned that dreams rarely come easily — but unwavering commitment, determination and perseverance can turn ambition into reality. *The Line Maker* illustrates that every small, intentional line becomes part of a greater masterpiece — the art of life and leadership itself. Never shackle your own feet. Never stop reaching for what seems impossible."

— **Joel Christopher Payne**, Disney Interpretive Gallery Artist

"There's an art to winning. As an NFL quarterback, I've lived at the line of scrimmage — where expectation meets resistance and nothing moves unless you do. *The Line Maker* shows what it really takes to drive toward the goal line of success: intention, execution, and the vision to find opportunity when others swear it isn't there."

— **Luke Falk**, NFL Quarterback and PAC-12 Record Holder

Published by Maison Vero
3002 Dow Avenue,
Suite 112 Tustin, CA 92780

Maison Vero is a professional publishing house that partners with rising authors to bring their thought leadership to the world. By respecting the copyright of an author's intellectual property, you enable Maison Vero and the author to continue publishing exceptional books for years to come. We thank you for supporting the author's copyright by purchasing an authorized edition of this book.

Inquiries may be directed to: Maison Vero, 13002 Dow Avenue, Suite 112 Tustin, CA 92780, or info@graymilleragency.com.

For information about special discounts for bulk purchases, please call 1-949-333-4872 or email info@graymilleragency.com.

Maison Vero is a partner brand of The Gray + Miller Agency a speaking, literary, and talent consortium.

For more information on the talent represented by The Gray + Miller Agency, or to bring any of our thought leaders to your organization or live event please visit our website at graymilleragency.com

Cover Design: Zach Sharples
Book Design: Mel Wise

Manufactured in the United States of America

Paperback 978-1-969508-07-3   E-book.   978-1-969508-09-7
Hardcover 978-1-969508-08-0

THE LINE MAKER

LIVE INTENTIONALLY. NO EXCUSES.

A Life Leadership Parable

BY BRETT ARMSTRONG

Dedicated to those ready to take up a new canvas.

To my wife, who leaves her mark with intention and love, and to my children, who bring adventure and color to my world.

Never be afraid to draw outside the lines.

PREFACE

I believe there is an art to a life well lived. It's an art mastered only by those who understand the true potential of intentional living, especially during times of uncertainty and change.

This magical allegory is specifically written for anyone who has faced an ending, encountered a new beginning, found themselves at a crossroads in life, or is simply seeking direction. Change is certain, as is the opportunity it brings — but only if you're ready to act and willing to shift your perspective.

Whether you're starting out, shifting careers, building a relationship, or leading through change — chances are, change is on the horizon.

Perhaps the only change you're confronting is a desire to grow. Whatever your circumstances, I encourage you to take up a new canvas. With that single act of courage, you unlock a gift of unlimited potential. It's then your responsibility to create the life you desire. It won't be easy — there will be challenges — but you can design a life that's truly your own.

When frustration sets in, remember this: Optimism is the artist of opportunity.

As you turn the pages, you'll encounter fictional characters facing change and explore the valuable lessons they learn as they embrace new opportunities. This story is a collection of principles and insights gathered from those who've mastered the art of living in an abstract and unpredictable world.

Regardless of where you stand in life — whether it's at the starting line, your heart brimming with the anticipation of a new adventure; or finding yourself nearing a finish line, with the wisdom of your journey behind you; or maybe somewhere in between — this book was written for you.

One line at a time, one canvas at a time, let's discover your next masterpiece together. May the principles in these pages guide your journey. I truly hope you discover the same transformative power of a line that I have.

CHAPTER 1

A BLANK CANVAS

There are two types of people: those who see the world for what it is, and those who see it for what it could be. Rick wasn't the latter. His world was built on numbers — clean, predictable, and exact. Bar charts and balance sheets didn't lie. It was when organizations drifted into the gray that things started to unravel.

To Rick, daydreaming was a waste of time. Imagination wasn't grounded in reality. Logic was his control, and control was everything — especially after losing so much just a few years earlier. That's why he didn't pay attention when he first noticed the closed-door meetings or heard the whispers he hadn't been included in. He reasoned it was just his imagination — an untrustworthy paranoia that went against the truth of the numbers.

The thought of losing his job never truly occurred to him — that his way of life could change so drastically in a single phone call; that his reality could be peeled back, like a wizard pulling back a curtain, revealing something entirely new.

And yet, here he was — sitting on the Great Lawn of Central Park, unwrapping a homemade sandwich, staring at a city that once felt like his to conquer.

The Manhattan skyline stretched before him, a familiar silhouette he had called home for the past decade. In his twenties, the city had represented the epitome of success, the pinnacle of ambition in the business world. Now, at thirty-six, he still saw it that way — but found himself questioning his place in it.

The loss of his wife, and now his job, left him adrift. Without Bridgette by his side, it was just Rick with a half-eaten sandwich and the shattered pieces of the dreams they had built together. He stared at the horizon, searching for answers.

Bridgette had been gone for two years. Her absence had left him hollow. She wasn't just his wife; she was his best friend, his compass. Memories of her flashed in his mind, and he clenched his jaw, pressing his lips together to suppress the tide of emotion threatening to surface. He couldn't afford to lose control — not now, not here. He needed to stay composed, at least for the next few hours.

His thoughts shifted. Funny how life always seemed to deliver exactly what he didn't want — right when he needed it most.

In fact, Rick's life had always felt like a string of near-misses. Success always felt within reach, only to slip through his fingers at the last moment. Time and again, he found himself stuck in the realm of mediocrity, chasing dreams that didn't fully materialize. Bridgette had been the one to ground him during those times, her optimism a soothing balance to his frequent frustration. She would remind him of how far they had come, how much they had overcome together.

Rick had spent his first eighteen years surviving poverty and the next eighteen years working to escape it. Shaped by his childhood, he had always been fiercely independent, starting work at fifteen and never relying on anyone for financial support. Raised by a single mother who struggled to make ends meet, he grew up keenly aware of how close they were to the edge. If he wanted an education or a better life, he knew he had to earn it himself. For Rick, this was how he took control. It was his way of ensuring he would never become a footnote in someone else's story.

For the most part, he felt he had succeeded. Since moving from Rigby, Idaho, he and Bridgette had found their New York experience to be very different from the gritty underbelly so many associated with the city.

He wasn't wealthy by Manhattan standards, but they'd built a comfortable life in a two-bedroom apartment on the Upper West Side. Locals called it the UWS, a term Rick had adopted with pride. When they first moved into the neighborhood, he remembered feeling like they had just stepped into a romcom.

The UWS offered the ideal New York experience, where the lines of culture and opportunity seamlessly intertwined. People from all walks of life called the tree-lined brownstone blocks home. That doesn't mean much to someone not living in New York, but as Rick learned, brownstone apartments were named for the brown sandstone building fronts commonly found on most blocks.

Broadway was the soul of their neighborhood, with the subway running beneath it and Central Park West providing an escape from work. Bridgette loved the boutiques on Columbus Avenue, calling them "charming" after outings with friends. Rick preferred the cozy cafes and restaurants that suited every occasion.

That period of his life felt like an eternity ago, stolen from Rick just as his late wife was by a drunk driver's careless acts. Her memory lingered heavily, accompanied by the haunting echo of the heart monitor's beeping in her final hours. He longed for her presence, wishing she could console him through his latest challenge.

In that chapter of life, Rick had found a sense of belonging and endless possibilities, making New York a place where he could truly flourish. But now, after Bridgette's death and his recent layoff, that sense of belonging felt distant — the city offering no solace. While others turned to noisy bars, Rick knew that wasn't for him. He had to find another way forward.

Now, here he was — two days had passed since the phone call from Human Resources — and the initial shock had faded. With sixty days of severance, he wasn't in immediate financial trouble, but the uncertainty weighed heavily. Rick didn't know where to start or even what he wanted to do as he approached midlife, newly unemployed. For the first time, he felt unsure how to navigate this unfamiliar reality. He knew confusion and worry were normal, but that didn't make it easier to face.

And yet, beneath the worry and uncertainty, one emotion caught him off guard: relief. As much as he hated to admit it, a small part of him felt freed — and that feeling scared him most of all.

Rick took a deep breath as he attempted to ground himself back in the present. He contemplated where he would go from here.

"Okay, get ahold of yourself. This process is just getting started. You'll figure it all out with time."

Amid a whirlwind of negative emotions, Rick understood the need to summon strength and maintain a positive outlook. He was determined to utilize this transitional period for self-renewal, securing a new job, and embarking on a fresh start, carefully planning his days with a newfound sense of purpose.

Armed with his cellphone, Rick carefully crafted a to-do list, prioritizing tasks that required immediate attention. At the top was collecting personal belongings from the office, dropping off dry cleaning, and scheduling a dentist appointment while he still had coverage. Between these mundane tasks, he considered how to tackle his resume, gather letters of recommendation, and compose cover letters — though that would come later.

Still, Rick couldn't ignore how much the job market had changed in the nearly ten years since his last search. Back then, face-to-face interviews were standard, and video chats were just gaining traction. Now, he wondered if wearing neckties to interviews even mattered anymore. The rise of remote work had blurred the lines of professionalism, with colleagues in sloppy T-shirts, unkempt hair, or even pajama bottoms during virtual meetings — an unthinkable sight in his former office life.

To this day, Rick took pride in maintaining a level of professionalism. Standing up from the lawn, he brushed off a few blades of grass and adjusted the neatly pressed dress shirt he'd chosen before lunch — a nod to his former routine. Faded jeans had replaced the slacks of his office days, paired with Oxford sneakers that struck a balance between casual and polished. His favorite sport coat was a small reminder of the standards he still held himself to, even now.

Rick noticed gray clouds gathering in the distance as he prepared to leave for the 86th Street-Central Park West station. He straightened his posture, determined to hold his head high. The world may have shifted to a more casual tone, but he wasn't ready to let go of what had made him successful — showing up, even when everything else felt like it was falling apart.

Over the years, he'd grown to appreciate the subway. It was only a short ride on the Southbound C train to Times Square, and in that time, he amused himself by guessing the destinations of his fellow passengers. Everyone had their own unique uniform. You had the private-equity guys with blue button-down dress shirts, most with a subtle pattern and expensive suit coat. There were empowered businesswomen dressed to the nines carrying their heels and Kate Spade purse while sporting their unlaced Nikes for a quick swap before entering the office. And, of course, the frequent low-key tourist with the cliché "I love NYC" T-shirt.

Still playing the game — guessing everyone's background — he got off the subway at the Times Square station and made his way outside. As Rick stepped out of the station, a cool breeze met him — brisk but not unexpected for early spring. The sky overhead had shifted. He glanced up. Gray clouds were now directly overhead, casting a muted haze over the city's usual shimmer.

A light rain began to mist.

This was the part of the journey he dreaded. Since the turn in the economy, the city had been hit hard by a growing homeless population. Most New Yorkers saw it as a rising blight on what was once considered a "cleaned up" NYC. Now, the situation stared every onlooker, businessperson, and tourist squarely in the face.

Although he had just a short three-minute walk from the Times Square station to the office building where he worked, it felt like an eternity. Rick remembered how aggressive many in the homeless camps had become, at times literally having to weave his way through the panhandlers.

He recalled one individual who carried a sign asking for money if he could make you laugh. He'd tell his best one-liner to the sucker who stopped. Most would give him a dollar or two out of pity, but rarely laughed.

Another had the audacity a few weeks before to tell Rick that he accepted Venmo when Rick tried to get by with the old "Sorry, I don't have any cash on me."

Today the homeless traffic was particularly light. He only saw two individuals within proximity to the office building where he was headed. From a distance, he couldn't help but think that the first individual looked out of place. She was a tall, slender woman with deep auburn hair that caught the late afternoon light and a warm, approachable smile. There was a quiet, mature confidence about her — an effortless style that blended flowing fabrics and understated jewelry. Her look carried a touch of boho chic, but it wasn't overly polished or trendy — it felt authentic, as if it reflected an inner vibrancy. Yet, something about her seemed out of place, a subtle discord that was hard to pin down.

She gave Rick a friendly smile as he approached. She didn't say anything but held up a cardboard sign. It had an unfinished look about it, and strangely, Rick couldn't help but feel the sign had been written just for him.

All the sign said was ME, written in all caps.

But what stood out even more was the unfinished letter E. Instead of a standard capital, it was made of three horizontal, parallel lines, unconnected on the left side. Each line varied in length — the shortest at the top, the second slightly longer, and the third the longest of all, stacked neatly beneath the others.

And if that weren't odd enough, something else lingered around the letters — tiny dots, scattered like debris across the cardboard.

At first glance, they looked like specks of dirt or drops of rain soaking into the surface. But the longer Rick stared, the more deliberate they seemed, forming a loose arc above the letters, tapering gently in the middle — like a flurry of snow caught mid-flight, or the faint static of an old television screen.

They weren't smudges. They'd been drawn — carefully, intentionally — with the same black marker as the rest of the sign.

As he continued walking, Rick's attention shifted back to the boho girl who held the sign. His glance met hers momentarily, and he couldn't help but be captivated by her brilliant emerald-green eyes. A polite smile formed on his lips as he passed, and he swore he caught a hint of sandalwood in the air. She was clearly not homeless, but still held the cardboard sign as many homeless would. No words were spoken, yet something was odd about the encounter.

Continuing down the street, Rick saw a second person — this one clearly living on the streets. Half hidden in the shadow of an abandoned building with graffiti behind him, the man was dressed more in line with what Rick had come to associate with New York's homeless population. He wore far more clothing than was needed for the current temperature. It was early spring, but the homeless man was dressed for winter — a very cold winter, it appeared. A shopping cart was piled high with blankets. Two large garbage bags were propped up on either side of the man, who squatted almost in a catcher's stance. In one hand, he held what appeared to be a plain white artist's canvas.

"Can you spare five dollars?" the vagrant called, looking up to Rick. As he did, the wrinkles in the man's weathered face pulled tightly together, almost pleading for help.

Rick tried to ignore him.

"Please sir, I just need five dollars for a line." The homeless man stood and held the blank canvas directly in front of Rick's face. The canvas appeared to have a single coat of white paint on it, but nothing else.

Rick had often wondered how people got to this point, homeless and living on the street, but the man's words said it all.

The words echoed, "I just need five dollars for a line." He's on drugs, Rick thought, remembering a documentary he had recently watched about Colombian drug cartels and addicts snorting lines of cocaine.

"Out of my way," Rick said as he stepped aside to avoid the man and his canvas. He continued on, pushed through the revolving door in front of him and entered the office building.

He wanted to make the trip quick, pick up his belongings, and hopefully avoid seeing any of his former coworkers.

Rick checked in with security and was led to the second floor, where Arnold from HR waited. A black-and-white cardboard bankers box sat on the desk, filled with Rick's personal belongings. Arnold, a pudgy man with thinning hair and a kind smile, had always been friendly—one of the few people who made the office feel a little more human.

"Hi Rick. I took the liberty of clearing out your office. Everything should be there." Arnold tried to avoid eye contact with Rick. Layoffs were never easy. It wasn't easy on the person being laid off, and Rick knew from experience it wasn't easy on the employees who were forced to share the bad news. "If you feel that anything is missing, just let me know and we'll track it down. I'll just need your key card for security," Arnold concluded.

Rick reached into his coat pocket and pulled out the key card that had granted him access to the building for so many years, along with a wadded up five-dollar bill he'd forgotten about. After giving Arnold the card, he shoved the five-dollar bill back into his pocket.

"Thanks, Rick. I just need to remind you of the noncompete agreement you signed upon hire and then get your final release by having you sign here on the dotted line."

Rick lifted a nearby pen, his eyes lingering on the signature block. The line he was about to sign felt like both a finish line and the start of something unknown. He exhaled, putting ink to paper, and completed the severance forms before offering Arnold a firm but polite handshake.

Grabbing the black-and-white bankers box, he felt the weight of more than just office supplies. His thoughts drifted to the woman and the homeless man. Some ended up on the streets through bad choices, but others—maybe many—had simply hit a streak of bad luck. Was this where it all started—an unexpected layoff?

Ready to leave, Rick noticed a new collection of raindrops on the revolving door as he exited the building and started back to the station. The storm and his frustration intensified as he walked, and he soon found himself directly in front of the homeless man, crouching against the wall. Before the homeless man could say anything, Rick slapped the five-dollar bill he had found in his pocket into the man's hand and continued to walk.

"Wait, wait!" The homeless beggar jumped up and shuffled after Rick, his voice cutting through the city noise. Rick didn't stop. "The deal was five dollars for a line." The rain began to fall harder.

Rick had enough. He spun around, his frustration spilling over. "Look, I don't know what you want. I gave you the five dollars..." He stopped mid-sentence.

"Here you go. Here's the line! That was the deal," the old man said, placing a plain white canvas carefully on top of the box in Rick's arms. His eyes sparkled with unsettling delight, and tufts of stark white hair on his balding head jutted skyward, as if charged with electricity.

"There's nothing on this!" Rick scoffed, glaring at the blank canvas. But as the words left his lips, a faint electric-blue glow shimmered across the surface of the canvas, vanishing as quickly as it appeared. He blinked, his pulse quickening.

The old man's grin widened, and he bounced on the balls of his feet, slapping his knee with glee. "Some people see only emptiness — others see everything!" he exclaimed, his voice rising above the rain that had begun to fall harder. It was now a downpour. Thunder cracked like a whip in the distance.

Rick shook his head, muttering under his breath. "Crazy old man. There's nothing there." Yet, his gaze lingered on the canvas, searching for the glow he had seen momentarily. He took a deep breath, trying to shake the unease building in his chest, and turned to walk away.

The rain further intensified, sheets of water soaking him as he turned around — colliding hard with someone hurrying by.

"Careful, kid — the storm's just starting. Choose your road carefully," the man murmured, steadying him with a firm hand. Rick looked up. The stranger had jet-black hair, a mechanic's shirt, and a name patch that read "Nando." The light-blue work shirt darkened as it collected heavy rain drops. Nando exhaled, his eyes flickering to the canvas. His tone wasn't harsh but weighty.

Rick shivered — a chill ran through him, but not from the rain. He already knew where he was headed. Before he could respond, the man was gone — lost in the city blurred by water and light.

"Just my luck," Rick grumbled. But deep down, he knew the night wasn't done with him yet. He then quickened his steps toward Bryant Park station.

Another rumble of thunder clapped. Then, behind him, the old man's voice cut through the storm.

"Remember, a blank canvas isn't a gift — it's an opportunity."

CHAPTER 2

INCLINES AND DECLINES

Rick's eyes burned as they opened to the bright morning light crawling through the blinds.

He hadn't slept well. His dreams were disrupted by brief flashes of electric-blue light and a faint, steady hum—the same glow he swore he'd seen radiating from the canvas in the rain. But each time he opened his eyes, the room was still. Silent. Pitch-black.

When he did sleep, he didn't find peace. His pillow pulled him back—not into dreams, but into the weight of his memory.

There was a heaviness he couldn't shake, like the pain of something unfinished, pressing on his chest. Maybe it was the disappointment of losing his job. Maybe it was Nando's ominous warning to choose the right road.

Whatever it was, it pulled him somewhere deeper—into a memory he hadn't touched in years.

Rick was an only child, but he felt more like a disappointment to his single mother. He suspected she saw him as a living reminder of his father—a man she never talked about, no matter how often Rick asked.

All he knew came from a single, reluctant line: "He was brilliant with numbers." Rick wasn't sure what that meant, but he clung to it, imagining a man he could emulate. He decided he'd become a great businessman or mathematician—not because he loved either, but because it gave him identity.

His mother, a petite blonde with Scandinavian roots, couldn't have been more different than the father he imagined. Every year on his birthday, she'd remind him how she'd been so certain that he'd be a girl, that she'd picked the name Astrid to honor their Viking heritage.

He remembered her describing the moment the doctor handed her a dark-haired, brown-eyed baby boy. She'd been caught off guard. Astrid wouldn't work. Then came the impatient nurse with a clipboard, waiting for a name to put on the birth certificate. His mother, flustered, scrambled for an answer.

"Uh... Rick. Astrick," she'd said, stitching together her best compromise.

As a child, Rick hadn't thought much of it. But as a teenager, he grew to resent the name. Teachers stumbled over it, and classmates laughed. He couldn't ignore how much it sounded like "asterisk."

His mother tried to make it better, explaining the Greek origin of asterisk. Asteriskos meant "little star."

"That's what you are, Ricky," she'd say. "My little star."

Rick hated it. He vowed never to be an afterthought — a footnote like an asterisk in someone else's story. From then on, he insisted on being called Rick.

The vivid memory shot Rick upright in bed. His mind reeled between the jumbled memories of his dream, the layoff, and the canvas. Combined, they made him fearful he'd become the very thing he swore he'd never be: an afterthought. Middle-aged, widowed, and alone, his career had been the one constant he could point to as progress — and now, even that was gone.

Rick rubbed his eyes, wishing it was all a bad dream. But it wasn't; his rain-soaked clothes crumpled on the floor confirmed everything. It was real. Too real.

And yet, the strangest part wasn't the canvas or even the electric-blue glow. It was the uncomfortable feeling in his chest — like something had been set in motion.

"That's stupid," Rick muttered, pushing the thought away.

But the feeling didn't go anywhere.

Instead, the quiet of the early morning pressed in around him as he moved through the small apartment. He headed to the kitchen, reaching for his usual breakfast routine — a couple pieces of toast and a glass of orange juice spiked with an energy drink. He had never liked the taste of coffee, and this had always been his go-to for an early-morning jolt.

As Rick took a sip, his gaze drifted over the counter — across the room — to the garbage can in the corner.

That's where he'd tossed the soaked canvas last night, still wet from the downpour. He'd convinced himself it was just some weird stunt by an old man with nothing better to do.

Then he froze, toast still halfway to his mouth.

The canvas wasn't blank anymore. It didn't glow like before. Something had changed.

A surge of disbelief washed over him as he rubbed his eyes, questioning reality. Just the night before, the canvas had been blank — a clean surface awaiting an artist's touch. But now, something was there.

In the center of the canvas, a faint, pale line stretched across the surface. It was thick. Horizontal. Subtle enough to question but too defined to ignore.

Rick set his toast down. His pulse quickened.

He'd used the canvas to shield his box of belongings during the storm — maybe water had soaked through. That had to be it. Or maybe the rain had washed away the top layer of paint to reveal something beneath.

He approached the garbage head-on to get a closer look at the canvas. Only now, the line was gone. He blinked — hard. Nothing. But he'd seen it. Carefully, he lifted the canvas from the trash. It was damp and smooth, but blank.

He ran a finger across where the ghostly line had appeared. Nothing. Not even a trace.

He held the canvas up to the light, turning it slowly, looking for texture or shadow — anything. But it was just as it had been the night before. Blank.

Rick clenched his eyes shut, willing the line to return — just to prove he wasn't imagining things.

This couldn't all be in his head. Or could it? Had he finally cracked?

Both impressed and unsettled, Rick carried the canvas across the room and placed it lengthwise on a shelf mounted to a plain brick wall. He stepped back a few feet. Still blank.

Curious, he moved a little to the right. For a moment, he thought he saw the line.

He shifted further. Closed his eyes hard. As his pupils readjusted, there it was — the same pale-gray horizontal line. The edges were still sharp, but the color had darkened. He stepped back toward the center. As he did, a spark of electric blue flickered across the canvas, like a dying neon sign — flashing, sputtering, then gone.

"What the...?" he whispered.

He started testing all angles — viewing from far to the left, squatting low, then pulling a stool over to check it from above. To his amazement, every vantage point offered a slightly different ghostly image of the horizontal line, as if waiting to be captured.

It didn't make sense. But he couldn't deny it. "Impossible," he whispered, but the word felt flat in the silence of the apartment.

For a second, he considered tossing it back in the trash, but something in him hesitated.

Instead, Rick walked over to the bankers box and pulled out a chisel-tipped permanent marker. He popped the cap off with his teeth. The sharp, chemical scent of the exposed marker drifted past his nose.

He stepped back to the canvas.

Holding the marker in a clenched fist, he pressed the tip firmly to the surface and dragged it from left to right, tracing the line he'd seen.

As soon as he lifted the marker, the room flashed electric blue — bright, fast, then gone again.

He stood there, breathing hard. The glow from the night before filled his mind again — vivid as the rain. He hadn't imagined it. He had seen it. Felt it.

And now, just like the line he'd drawn, it was real.

But what was the purpose of the line? If it held a secret, he couldn't decipher it. All he knew was that he had acquired what he thought was a blank canvas for a mere five dollars, unaware of the profound impact it now had on his perception of reality — or his sanity.

He stared in awe and disbelief as the room fell into stillness, and the canvas seemed to hum with its own presence.

"Not bad for five bucks," Rick muttered with a faint grin, his eyes fixed on the canvas.

But the grin faded as the old man's words echoed again: "Some people see only emptiness — others see everything." The phrase dug in, refusing to let go.

Rick leaned back against the wall, still staring at the canvas.

Something about it made him uneasy — not just what it showed, but what it stirred. The line he'd seen. The flickers. The way it seemed to change depending on how he looked at it.

An unsolicited thought crept to the surface, "What if he'd been looking at everything the wrong way?"

Rick pivoted to the far-right corner of the room, eyes locked on the canvas.

The thick black line was no longer alone. It had shifted to the bottom edge, and above it, smooth, fluid lines began to take shape — graceful curves rising and falling in succession.

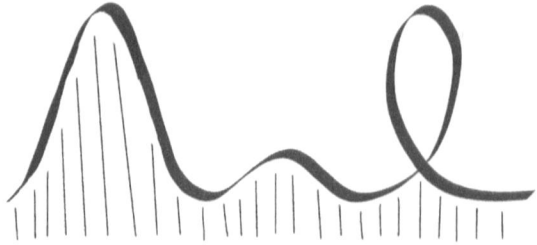

Rick blinked, certain his mind was playing tricks again.

The linework looked calculated, like it had been drawn with a calligraphy pen. The arcs and valleys tapered cleanly, forming rolling waves. Beneath them, the black line held steady — a foundation beneath motion.

Rick leaned forward, heart racing. It was a roller coaster.

The image hit too close to home — the ups and downs mirrored exactly what he was living.

The past few years had been brutal. Lately, he'd wished to erase the extremes — to level them out, find quiet. Just stop the ride.

Then it hit, that mix of dread and anticipation, like the slow climb before a drop.

He could feel it. The clatter. The tension. That split second before gravity took over. Life felt like that now. Not a fall. Not a rise. A transition.

He exhaled. The hum of the present settled around him. For a fleeting second, he could almost smell the hot grease of an old wooden coaster.

Then the lines shifted, and the curves sharpened. The shape transformed again. Rick stared, holding his breath. He recognized it instantly — a heartbeat. An EKG rhythm.

He'd seen that line before — when his wife passed. And years before that, with his mother.

A wave of shame rolled through him. Wanting to flatten the peaks and valleys? That wasn't peace. It would be death. A flatline was the end.

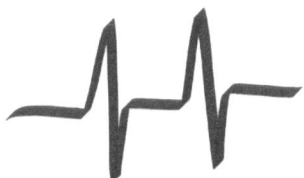

He stared at the canvas, caught between fear and fascination. That's the thing with life — and roller coasters. Sometimes you can't tell where the fear ends and the thrill begins.

Then, as if daring him forward, the canvas pulsed — just once — with that same electric-blue glow.

Rick didn't move. Whether it was an invitation or a warning, he didn't know. But one thing was certain: He couldn't ignore it. Not anymore.

CHAPTER 3

PICK UP THE QUILL

For over a week now, Rick had wandered the city, retracing his steps through Manhattan in search of the homeless man who'd sold him the canvas or the boho girl he'd seen that day in the rain.

Faces of strangers blurred together, but no matter how many streets he walked, parks he visited, or benches he passed, they were nowhere to be found.

Deep down, he knew the search wasn't just about them. It was about the canvas and the strange spell it had on him. He couldn't explain it, but it felt like a riddle demanding resolution—a puzzle with missing pieces he was desperate to find.

Now, after another long day of wandering, the golden-yellow sun was setting in the distance, casting a blood-orange glow on the underside of the clouds that hung over New York City. Rick had checked off the mundane errands on his list, though he knew they were merely a front for his true intention. The streets around him buzzed with their usual energy, but he wandered aimlessly, lost in his thoughts.

The canvas, still sitting on the shelf in his apartment, haunted him. Its black lines, so simple yet deliberate, lingered in his mind, impossible to ignore. He didn't know why, but he was certain the answers would find him, just as the canvas had.

Then he stopped.

Rick's gaze dropped to the ground, his eyes widening. There, on the sidewalk before him, lay an exact replica of the thick line he had first seen on the canvas. But unlike the horizontal line back home, this one was jet-black and stretched lengthwise across the concrete slab in the direction he was walking, as if guiding him forward.

The paint appeared fresh — a gleaming wetness in the dying light of the day — as though someone had just placed it there. Curious, Rick dragged his toe across the pavement, smudging the line slightly underfoot. The paint was still wet, not yet fully dry.

Rick looked up, his head on a swivel, hoping to find the street artist who had painted it. He didn't see anyone who fit the profile. He scanned his surroundings, searching for anything or anyone that could explain its presence. But the ordinary strangers just passed by, their hurried footsteps oblivious to what Rick saw.

This was no coincidence. He took a tentative step forward, following the line with his eyes as questions buzzed in his mind. How had it appeared here, in this exact place? Why now? The more he stared at it, the more certain he became. The line wasn't random.

Rick exhaled slowly and moved forward, his curiosity outweighing his apprehension. The line seemed to beckon him — a silent invitation to uncover what lay ahead. Somehow, he knew this was only the beginning.

Then he saw her, in the distance and long shadows of dusk, the faint silhouette of the boho girl walking away with her back toward him.

This was it. All day he'd been searching blindly. He hadn't known where to begin. The city had seemed so large and intimidating. Now, all at once, he had direction. For the first time in a week, he felt guided by a line that wasn't supposed to be there. He sprinted to the end of the street corner where he had seen her. He looked in all directions, but she was nowhere to be found. He turned right, just as he had watched her do. Still no sign, but just a few feet away, centered perfectly on the concrete slab, was the same freshly painted line.

Rick followed, continuing the process for blocks. He never saw the girl — only followed the series of dashed lines like a trail on a paper map, leading the follower to their destination. Only the boho girl knew where that destination was.

Though he followed the lines, he did so carefully, making sure to stay alert. He continually looked for any signs of danger. Cautiously, he sidestepped through a foreboding alley before reaching a warehouse with a warm, flickering light above the doorway. The sputtering light faintly illuminated a solid, singular, thick black line painted horizontally across the matte-gray door. Rick had never seen the building, and he didn't know this area of town existed. Now what?

Rick debated whether or not to knock, but decided instead to cautiously open the door. He peeked inside but couldn't have imagined what he would find. His mind was conflicted. Should he or should he not be there?

The sprawling warehouse was unlike anything he'd ever seen. It was filled with strange, colorful, and mysterious paintings. Many were still on easels, some propped against the wall, and others filed away like books on towering warehouse racks that lined the outer walls, at least two stories high. Most of the canvases were massive, too large for any one person to carry comfortably by themselves. Others were small and nearly blank.

It felt like stepping into a fantastical library, and Rick was overcome with awe and wonder. Only the colors bleeding onto the edges of each canvas were visible on the warehouse racks — like the spines of magical books waiting to be read. Each painting stood side by side, but collectively, the exposed edges formed an abstract image — a vibrant, hidden story told in fragments. It was a collective work of many artists.

Rick could tangibly feel some kind of energy pulsing in the air. He stepped into the warehouse, quietly shut the door, and walked around, exploring the strange works of art. With each step, he marveled at the canvases around him. He felt the emotions of every brush stroke from every artist. At times he felt embarrassed, as if he were looking into the private life of the painter. He felt emotions with each brush stroke, paint splatter, and line on every canvas.

He found admiration for both the completed works as well as the canvases that held no color; these were early in development, many consisting of only a few sketched lines.

He wandered around, examining his surroundings, completely unaware that he was being watched. He wasn't alone. It was as if they had expected him.

"Welcome! You finally made it!" The words frightened Rick. He was so lost in the energy and paintings that he hadn't noticed anyone else in the room.

Rick spun around and was greeted by a wild-eyed old man, with tufts of stark white hair standing upright around the perimeter of his head. He had poked his head around the side of a massive canvas he was working on so that Rick could see him. He gave kind of an open-mouthed smile as if to shout, "Surprise!" Rick was beyond surprised because, though better kept, it was the same homeless man who had sold him the blank canvas on the street corner.

If he hadn't known better, Rick could have sworn it was Doc Brown staring back at him. Doc Brown was one of Rick's favorite characters from the movie *Back to the Future*. As a teen, Rick had watched it dozens of times.

"Doc, is that you?" Rick quoted the movie.

"Marty!" The wild-eyed old man played along, then stepped out from behind the canvas where he worked. "I get that a lot. People say I look like Doc Brown. I personally don't get it," the stranger said emphatically, but with a heavy Italian accent.

But Rick saw it, the likeness to Doc was uncanny. In addition to his wild, energetic eyes and crazy hair, the elderly man wore a white lab coat splattered with paint over an untucked red Hawaiian shirt. A pair of round, wire-rimmed glasses were propped up high on his head, but would have been better placed on his large and pointed nose.

"Actually, my name is Eldon, but you can call me El. Ready to get started?" His eyes sparkled as he flashed a big, open smile with his arms outstretched in dramatic flair. He acted as if he had known Rick his entire life.

"Ready for what?"

"Are you ready to begin your masterpiece, Rick?"

"What are you talking about? I don't know how to paint. How do you know my name?" Rick was actually a little spooked.

The bottom of El's paint-splattered lab coat flew back as he dashed across the warehouse to retrieve an artist's blank sketch pad.

"Never mind that, Rick." He had the audacity to say his name again. "None of that is important right now, and I never said anything about painting. We're going to start simple. We always start simple with an apprentice."

Rick's heart raced as he stared at El in disbelief. Again, how could this stranger know his name? What did he mean by starting simple with an apprentice? Losing his job, Rick already felt vulnerable. Was he being taken advantage of? The unexpected conversation sent shivers down his spine.

El, unrattled by Rick's confusion, swiftly returned with the blank sketch pad from the messy warehouse. The paint splatters on his lab coat danced as he moved. "Don't worry about that now, Rick," El attempted to assure him, though his voice still carried an air of mystery. "Forget everything you are thinking right now. Let go of the anger and the frustration. Just breathe."

Rick's skepticism wrestled with his curiosity. He couldn't ignore the fact that this encounter seemed to be more than coincidence. Their prior meeting on the street, the blank canvas, and the lines that led him to the warehouse told him there must be purpose in the adventure. Rick took a deep breath and decided to listen.

"All right," he said, his voice laced with a mix of frustration and intrigue. "What is this all about? Why am I here?"

With a knowing smile, El began, his words now carrying a weight of life experience and wisdom. "That's the real question, isn't it Rick? Why are you here? Why am I here? Why are any of us here? Life is unpredictable. Sometimes it takes unexpected encounters and unconventional paths to discover our true potential. It's all about the masterpiece."

"Look, my life was just upended! I have no idea what you are talking about! Why did you give me that canvas?" He shook his head, frustrated by the old man.

"I know! I know, Rick. We have so much to talk about. But I need you to trust me. We need to talk about the lines you have been seeing. Have you heard of Samuel Smiles?"

Rick didn't trust him. He had no reason to. He froze for a moment.

"No, I haven't heard of Samuel Smiles," Rick said, hesitantly.

"He was quite the character, Rick, though most people have never heard of him. He came from very humble means. He lived in the 1800s, and his family were linen weavers. Think about that, Rick — they wove every line of thread to create linen." El paused in reflection.

"That's how Samuel approached life," El said, his eyes glinting with enthusiasm. "Building line by line." He paused, motioning toward a nearby piece of art, its intricate lines intertwining in a calculated pattern. "He believed in the transformative power of character and perseverance."

Rick furrowed his brow, glancing between El and the artwork. The old man's words hung in the air, carrying a weight that seemed to resonate beyond the room.

"Even though Samuel started out from very humble means," El continued, his hand tracing an invisible line in the air, "he improved himself to become a doctor. But that wasn't enough. That was before he started his real work as a writer."

El stepped closer to Rick, his gaze sharpening. "He literally became the creator of the first self-help book. His most famous work was called *Self-Help*, written in 1859. It was a blueprint for life."

Rick tilted his head, his curiosity piqued. "A blueprint?"

El nodded, his tone unwavering. "He believed people had untapped potential. Believed that success required rolling up your sleeves, putting in the work, and making things happen." The old man's hand rested briefly on the edge of the canvas, as if to emphasize his point.

"He believed we learn through our experiences. And let's face it, you can't have new experiences if you just go around in circles, never trying anything new."

Rick leaned back slightly, the weight of the words sinking in. The old man's passion was infectious, and for a moment, Rick felt the pull of something larger, a quiet challenge he wasn't sure he was ready to face.

El paused once again, looked up, and motioned to the door that Rick entered from. Above the door was a carefully stenciled quote.

"The apprenticeship of difficulty is one which the greatest of men have had to serve." – Samuel Smiles

"You're trying to survive change, Rick," El said, his voice cutting through the silence. "But what you need to do is embrace it. Life doesn't give you experiences just to endure — they're meant to awaken your ability to create. The greatest artists find beauty even in ugliness. Sometimes it takes time to see, but it's always there, waiting to be found. Difficulty draws the line when we don't want to. Difficulty can be a catalyst to discover, to create."

El's voice grew firmer, his hand gesturing toward Rick with pointed intent. "That's why you're here. You were meant to create!"

He let silence linger before adding, "Our actions are like lines on a canvas — each one leaves a mark, contributing to the overall picture of our lives."

Rick nodded as El stepped closer, his tone softening but losing none of its intensity. "I know what you're going through, Rick, but you're in good company. Life isn't easy, and no one's getting out of here alive. As for the canvas, I didn't give you anything. You bought it." He tapped his temple with one finger, as if sharing a vital secret. "And that's important."

El stepped back, clasping his hands behind his back, his gaze distant yet purposeful. "In fact, it's the first lesson of the apprenticeship."

Rick was still confused. "The first lesson? An apprenticeship?"

"Yes, the first lesson is this: Life can quite literally be an apprenticeship in difficulty. You'll be given challenges — some to help you grow, others to awaken a strength or purpose you didn't know was there."

Rick hesitated, torn between leaving and staying. The strange occurrences and mysterious lines since picking up the canvas couldn't be mere coincidence. His curiosity won out and he decided to press on.

"Did you bring the canvas?"

"Uh, no... I didn't," Rick hadn't known he'd end up here at the studio.

"Okay, no problem. We'll get there. But for now, we're just going to practice." El opened the cover of the large spiral-bound sketch pad he had retrieved earlier and tossed it down on a butcher-block table in front of Rick.

The table was one of several dozen scattered about the massive warehouse. Four high metal stools surrounded each table. Both the tables and stools had fallen victim to random spills of ink and drips of colored paint, over what Rick assumed were years of use. Each unlikely mark gave them character.

"Before we begin," El said, "there's something foundational — something else you need to understand: the blank canvas."

El paused, studying Rick's face to make sure the point landed.

"In this studio, you have access to an unlimited number of canvases," he continued, "but it's up to you to decide when you're ready for a new one. Only you can make that choice."

El's tone softened slightly as he went on. "Sometimes a project will come to a natural end, and you'll know your work is done. Other times, unforeseen circumstances may force the canvas to close before you're ready. In those moments, you must consciously choose to start anew.

"I want you to imagine that your life is nothing more than a wide, open canvas — pure white, waiting."

Rick pictured himself standing before it — a massive stretch of untouched possibility, trembling with unlimited potential.

El continued, "This canvas has an undiscovered future. By taking it, you make a conscious decision to create, to shape your own story. It's an act of courage, exploring and embracing the unknown. The only limits are the edges of the canvas, your imagination, and your willingness to work."

As Rick listened, he began to realize the depth of El's wisdom. The canvas was not just about art, it was about life itself. Perhaps they were one and the same.

"Rick, are you paying attention?" El's voice broke into his thoughts. Rick nodded, more mindful now.

"Every canvas is like a new season of life," El said, his voice steady but brimming with energy. "A new chapter in a magnificent work of art."

Rick glanced toward a blank canvas resting against the wall, the words settling over him like a weight he couldn't yet define.

"But it doesn't just unfold before you — not the great ones, anyway," El continued. He stepped closer, his hand gesturing toward the empty space in front of them. "Taking the canvas must be done with intention and resolve. It means stepping forward, Rick, grasping opportunity with both hands and committing to the journey ahead."

Rick shifted his weight, his mind churning with unspoken questions. "And what if I don't know where to start?" he asked, his voice barely above a whisper.

El smiled, a knowing look in his eyes. "That's the thing about a blank canvas. Sometimes you just need to be bold enough to begin. The canvas will show you."

El turned, motioning around the studio. "This is true for everyone — artists, business owners, parents, children, and yes, even writers staring at unwritten chapters. In that new beginning, Rick, a future awaits."

Rick began to understand more clearly. "So that's what I bought when I gave you five dollars that day in the rain?"

El became overly animated. "Oh, Rick, you bought so much more. It wasn't about the five dollars — that was just a symbol of your decision to embrace a new beginning. Every new beginning requires something in return. Every fresh start requires a sacrifice — time, money, effort, or even leaving behind what no longer serves you. Every new canvas has a price. I don't set it and you don't set it. The price is determined by the potential of the canvas."

"So, to live boldly, one must be willing to sacrifice and embrace the unknown," Rick said aloud, confirming his understanding.

In his realization, he heard the low, electric-like hum of the canvases. All around the perimeter of the warehouse, canvases on easels, shelves, and tabletops gave off the same electric, neon-blue glow that he had seen earlier.

"What is that?" Rick asked, sensing that El also recognized it.

"Congratulations, Rick — you've discovered your first truth. Truth resonates throughout the universe, and when we recognize it, it can be magical. It echoes through the works of our lives. Never forget what you've just learned: Every canvas has a price. Every opportunity requires a sacrifice of some type. It could be anything. Now, let's begin!"

Rick wasn't exactly sure what he had gotten himself into, but the prospect of personal growth and self-discovery ignited a spark of hope within him.

"Now, I want you to do something for me," El motioned to the sketch pad on the table and pushed it closer to Rick. "This will be your canvas."

"Let me guess, draw a line?" Rick asked, thinking back to the many references to lines in his recent life.

"Precisely! How did you know?" El exclaimed, his eyes wide. "Go on! Go on! Sit down." El didn't give Rick time to respond.

But Rick didn't bother to sit down. He picked up a nearby pencil, leaned over the sketch pad, and was just about to scrawl a line across its page, when El gasped and frustratedly shook his head, waving his arms as if to ward off smoke or some great evil about to be unleashed.

"What are you doing?" El's voice was urgent yet gentle. He knew Rick couldn't be expected to understand — at least not yet. "First rule of

Zivot Studio: You don't just grab a cheap pencil and start drawing on a whim. What we do here matters. Every line, every choice.

"Here, take this," El said, handing Rick suitable replacements.

Rick examined the two elegant objects closely — a dark-glass bottle of ink, shimmering with an otherworldly glow, and what appeared to be a slender dip pen. He turned the pen over in his hands, feeling its weight and balance. It had the unmistakable feel of an antique.

Skeptically, he voiced his observation, "Seriously? A quill pen?"

El's lips curled slightly, indicating a small smile. "Not quite," he corrected. "This is a dip pen, not a quill. A true quill pen was made of an actual feather. The Industrial Revolution did away with the quill pen, and in its place, steel nibs like this emerged." El gestured to the small metal blade that had been inserted into the contoured wooden handle.

To Rick, it seemed like a minor technicality — quill pen, dip pen, whatever. Either way, the technology felt ancient.

Rick's eyebrows raised. "Wouldn't it be easier just to use the pencil?"

Rick hadn't finished his thought before El interrupted. "My boy, nothing worth doing is easy," the heavily accented words were sincere. "If you want easy, walk out of my door and join the rest of the world."

Rick considered it. He still didn't know why he was there; he just knew he was supposed to be. Life had brought him to this place. An unexpected electrical pulse, like a miniature blue lightning bolt inside the dark-glass ink bottle, seemed to confirm his thought.

"Everything we do in Zivot Studio has a purpose. Every one of my pupils begins with a dip pen and ink. There's a time and a place for a pencil, just not now. You must learn to be deliberate," El held up his hand to stifle any argument from Rick.

"Unlike a pencil, the ink doesn't just come to you, you must take it. You must draw it up into the nib, just like the courage and creativity life will require. You must be intentional in your approach and let the masterpiece flow from you. The pen is an extension of who you are."

Rick shrugged, uneasy with the eccentric approach. He wasn't used to the artist's world. In his own world, it was all about efficiency and getting the job done.

"Now, I'm going to ask you to draw a line, like the ones you followed to get here. Picture it in your mind," El said.

"So you know about the lines I've been seeing?"

"Of course I do. Lines are all around us!" El scolded him, but then took a deep breath, an effort to find his Zen. "Hold the pen so that it feels comfortable to you. Hold it so that your wrist can move freely."

El then made a slight adjustment to Rick's grip. "Lightly, don't kill it. "

Rick remembered golf lessons from his grandfather, where he instructed him to hold the club with the same pressure that he would a baby bird. Strong enough that it couldn't get away, but not so tight that it harmed the bird.

"There, now when you're ready, dip the tip of the nib into the inkwell. Get just enough that it catches in the blade. Get too much and it will be a mess. Then as you place the tip on the surface, the ink will naturally flow out."

Rick did his best to follow the old man's instructions. After dipping the "nib," as the old man called it, he carefully lifted the pen from the ink, watching as a bead of ink formed just above the tip.

Trying his best, Rick held the pen above the sketch pad and tried to envision the perfect line, which he would pull across the page from left to right.

He waited just a moment too long. With too much ink on the nib, a large drip fell from 3 to 4 inches above the paper, leaving an irregular star-shaped blemish.

Rick hesitated, but reasoned that it was just practice, and so he placed his pen to the paper and pulled a neat, semi-straight line.

"Beautiful!" the wild-eyed old man exclaimed.

"It's awful," Rick retorted back. "Look at it."

"It's not awful, Rick. It was your first try and it will become the center of your masterpiece. At Zivot, we use ink to remind us that every action in life is permanent and we embrace it, even our mistakes in our art. It's how we learn."

"Really?" Rick murmured. "What's so great about a line? Why would I want that at the center of my masterpiece? Look at the big splotch!"

"Oh, Rick, that's where you have it all wrong. A line can be anything and it can be everything. It has the power to turn nothing into something! Lines are a simple thing, but they are powerful. Lines are what we make them. Drawn wrong, and they'll make you sad. Drawn right, and they'll make you glad."

El took the quill from Rick's hand and with the precision of a surgeon drew two curved lines, exactly the same length — one drawn in a bend to indicate a frown, the other in the shape of a smile.

"So which is it? Is it a smile or a frown?" Rick asked.

El continued, "Let me say it again. Lines have the power to transform nothing into something. Lines on a blank page can literally create a masterpiece."

Rick thought back to the blank canvas in his apartment, remembering how the first line that appeared had immediately captured his attention.

"You can lay down the line. You can pick up the line. You can stand in line and complain, or stand in line to experience the ride of your life."

"But what is the line? Is it a smile or a frown?" Rick asked again.

El elaborated, "Aww, that's an interesting question. It can be whatever you want it to be. How do you choose to view it? How do you choose to see your experiences? Was your layoff an ending or a new beginning? It's untapped opportunity and potential. It's whatever you choose to make it, Rick — even your mistakes. This might be the most important line you can learn. It's the line of interpretation."

"Line of interpretation?" Rick asked.

As Rick said the words, the two curved lines El had drawn just moments before began to radiate the electric-blue glow that Rick was beginning to recognize.

"That's right, Rick. Does that surprise you? The way we interpret things is a very fine line, it can be fragile. The way you interpret or define even a very small event can be the difference between success and failure. And since you get to define your marks, you might as well define them in ways that work to your benefit."

El paused, the nib poised above the ink bottle. Selecting an 8- x 10-inch piece of artboard to serve as his canvas, he set aside the sketch pad — it wouldn't suffice for a lesson this important. Dipping the nib into the ink, he deliberately drew up more than needed.

Carefully, he positioned his hand over the left side of the artboard, perfectly centered from top to bottom. The canvas, oriented in a landscape fashion, remained steady beneath his hand. For a moment, he held still, allowing gravity to pull the ink to the nib's tip. Rick watched as the ink gathered into a bead before falling to the surface, creating a star-shaped splotch.

It resembled Rick's earlier mistake, but El studied it with something closer to curiosity than criticism. There was no hesitation, no sign of disapproval — only the quiet certainty of someone who saw something more. As if, to him, the mark wasn't a flaw at all, but potential. A chance for meaning, no matter how small.

"You see, Rick, what you saw as a blemish, I see as a creative spark," El said, letting the idea settle — firmly planting itself in Rick's brain.

"Rick, every aspect of our life originates from a single spark. Whether that is a creative spark, the spark of love, the spark of inspiration, or the spark of life, it is the magical moment of conception. The Great Creator allows us to be part of that undefined opportunity. From there, every opportunity has a lifeline that is in your control. A line, like everything, has a start and a stop. It has a beginning and an end." As he spoke, his hand worked like a surgeon.

Using the "spark" as a starting point, El drew out a straight consistent line, followed by a small series of peaks and valleys. He then drew another short uninterrupted span, and once again a sequence of peaks and valleys, concluding with a final straight stretch of line. It was a representation of the life that could be given to the opportunity.

"Wait, that's the same image I saw the other day!" As Rick reviewed El's creation, he realized it was identical to the cardiac axis — the heart rhythm that had formed on his canvas the day after he bought it.

The old man ignored him, not ready to answer all of the questions in Rick's mind. Instead, El turned his eyes and surveyed the room. Rick could feel the energy and the artistry stronger than ever. Each piece of art seemed to radiate its own energy.

"Every one of these works of art once started as a single stroke," El motioned around the room. "That first stroke was the first time inspiration began to take physical form. No two lines or strokes are ever identical. As the artist, it's your job to give that spark a lifeline — to keep it alive. Because if you don't, it fades. Forgotten before it ever had a chance to exist."

El appeared intoxicated by the energy and life in the room. "Rick, tonight this is your beginning. You've been given an opportunity to make your mark. Never underestimate the simplicity or the power of a line. Never underestimate the power of just beginning."

He finished with a question only Rick could answer: "What will you create?"

CHAPTER 4

MISALIGNED EXPECTATIONS

Rick awoke in a daze. Though he'd slept well, he felt unrested; his mind had been piecing together his late-night conversation with El. He hadn't planned to spend hours discussing lines with a stranger, but the encounter had shifted something in him, bending time and opening his mind to new possibilities.

As he lay in bed, staring at the ceiling, vivid memories of the studio lingered — the warm energy, the self-illuminated canvases. His ink-stained hand tugged the comforter closer as rain pattered outside. One moment replayed vividly — El's parting words: "Never underestimate the simplicity or the power of a line. Never underestimate the power of just beginning." El's intense gaze had been unmistakable; he wanted Rick to understand.

Rick laughed, he didn't even know what El meant. He still wasn't sure how there was power in a line. The simplicity made sense, but where was the power?

At that moment, Rick committed to finding out. Curiosity seemed to pull him from the warm covers as he crawled out of bed. Thinking back on the night, he realized he had been overdressed. Today he decided to dress for the occasion.

After showering, he grabbed a pair of jeans and a white T-shirt. His ink-stained hand removed the T-shirt from its hanger. It didn't matter how hard he had scrubbed, his hand wouldn't come clean. It reminded him of grade school art class, coming home covered in magic marker.

Ricked grabbed a bagel from the counter and approached the door to begin his journey back to the unusual studio, where El promised he would be waiting. Rick was curious about what the day's events would reveal.

As he began to exit his apartment, he passed the white canvas hanging on the wall.

But the original horizontal line with the tapering end was no longer alone. At its far edge was a bold ink blot, followed by a semi-straight line — his original line.

The inkblot was the same mark Rick had made the night before during his failed attempt to draw a straight line with ink and nib.

Perplexed, he paused, staring intently at the altered image.

Why was his mistake now part of the canvas?

He had to find out what it meant.

Rick followed the same path he had the day before, but the journey felt endless.

It reminded him of being a kid — how time always seemed to crawl in the days leading up to the holidays or a long-awaited family vacation.

As he walked, he couldn't help but notice every line along the way. His time with El last night made him notice things he'd never paid attention to before. He noticed white and yellow lines in the street, people standing in lines for breakfast, and picket lines with upset workers. Just as El had said, the lines became whatever the participants intended.

As he ventured farther, the aroma of freshly roasted coffee embraced him, weaving through the air and filling it with warmth. It was a stark contrast to the stank odors of the bustling city streets, where the steam rising from the grates and manholes mingled with the brisk springtime air.

The scent of the coffee, carried with it a promise of rejuvenation — a reminder that among the harsh realities of the city, there existed opportunities for new beginnings. It awoke memories of quaint cafes and bustling markets of the city he once loved.

Finally, he arrived at the studio. The dark alley he had entered yesterday was not nearly as intimidating in the daylight.

Approaching the door, Rick did a double take.

The matte-gray surface was no longer marked by a single horizontal line. In its place was a new image — one he had seen earlier that morning. His ink-blotted attempt to draw a line.

Only now, he couldn't shake the feeling that it resembled a lowercase i.

His attention was drawn from the stenciled image to the thin gap around the door. The area between the door and the door frame was not airtight. Rick could see the same electric-blue glow that radiated from the paintings last night. Its intensity was so strong that he could see it even in the daylight hours, beaming out around the door.

Opening it, he stepped in and instinctively closed his eyes. His body was enveloped in the warm, electric glow of the paintings throughout the studio. He didn't need to see it, he felt it. He exhaled a comfortable sigh as the light bathed him.

"Amazing, right? That's how I feel every time I come here." A confident feminine voice brought Rick to the present.

He jolted to attention, surprised. It wasn't El.

"Hi, Rick! I was wondering when you'd get here. El has a full day lined up for you."

Still startled, he opened his eyes to see the woman who had held the cardboard sign in the rain — the boho girl. As their eyes met, Rick was captivated. Something about her style was so unique. Though she was very close to Rick's age, maybe older, she exuded a youthful vibrance. She had a timeless confidence. It was an interesting combination: her age plus the energy of someone younger. Rick had known other people like this, those who seemed to age more gracefully than others. She had clearly won the game of genetic roulette, though he guessed she might have been in her late thirties.

"Oh, hello!" Rick said, studying her inquisitively. He had expected El, but the sight of her caught him off guard.

She laughed at his disbelief. "Sorry, I guess El didn't warn you it would be me today."

"Warn me? You knew I was coming? Are you always here?" Rick was full of questions.

"I'm not always here. I guess we have a way of showing up when the canvas calls," she replied, stepping closer.

Rick's pulse quickened.

She continued, trying to put his mind at ease, seemingly sensing his nerves. "I get it, we've all been there. Getting picked for the apprenticeship can be intimidating. Lines start to appear when you least expect them."

"Apprenticeship?" Rick had, for a moment, forgotten El's mention of it. The word felt heavier now — like a role he hadn't planned to step into.

She gave a small nod, as if that answered everything. "El asked me to get you started. Let's do that, and I'll tell you what I can. Come over here."

She stepped out from behind the canvas and easel where she'd been working, and walked over to the table where Rick's sketch pad waited. It was exactly where he had left it, along with the nib and ink.

"Your assignment is to make straight lines. You can stop when you've perfected it."

"Perfected it?" Rick asked.

The boho girl just laughed, "You'll know when you've got it."

It seemed like a strange request.

Rick sat down and dipped the nib in the dark-black ink. Learning from last night's mistake and ink splatter, he was careful not to get too much ink. Time after time, he attempted to draw a straight line. Rick quickly found that he had a tendency to raise the pen too quickly from the paper and the line tapered out rather than maintaining a consistent stroke.

He continued, this time concentrating harder.

Rick had filled many pages with various lines. When the boho girl pulled up a stool beside him, he glanced up to see her soft smile, warm and inviting, as she watched him work. A faint blend of sandalwood and vanilla lingered in the air, wrapping around him like a subtle, calming presence.

"So, Rick…" she started, but he interrupted her.

"That's really not fair. How do you know my name and why don't I know yours?"

"My name is Alma," she said, with a shrug and a grin.

"And that was you on the street corner in the rain by my office, right?" Rick asked. "Why were you there?"

"That's a conversation for another time," she said. "What do you know about Verrocchio?"

"Verrocchio?" Rick asked, confused. He only looked up briefly from his sketch pad, deep in focus.

"That's what I thought," Alma paused. "Most people haven't heard of him either, but if it weren't for Verrocchio, the world may not be what it is today. Verrocchio isn't a household name, but his pupil, Leonardo da Vinci is. I'm sure even you have heard of da Vinci."

Rick just rolled his eyes.

"Leonardo's father recognized at a young age that his son was gifted. He was a once-in-a-generation artist, and his father felt it was his responsibility to nurture that talent. So he sent his son to Florence to study under Verrocchio, who mentored him. He asked him to do things that seemed ridiculous."

Rick scoffed, "Like drawing lines until perfection?"

"Exactly like that, Rick," Alma explained, her eyes lighting up. "Have you seen *The Karate Kid*?"

"Sure, everyone has," Rick replied, this time putting the nib down to stretch his hand that had begun to cramp.

"Remember 'Wax on, wax off'?" asked Alma.

"And 'Paint the fence' and 'Sand the floor.'" Rick mimed the motions from another of his favorite movies.

Alma laughed. "Anyone who has ever studied under a master has probably been asked to do something that didn't make sense. That's why mentors are so powerful; they have a different perspective than the pupil being taught. They have experience and know what steps need to be taken to guide their apprentice."

"So El thinks I'm going to be a great artist? He's mentoring me?" Rick was doubtful.

"Yes, but maybe not in the way you are thinking. That will come with time. The truth is, he sees greatness in everyone. We're all capable of a masterpiece, but few take the time to understand how to create it. It takes time, patience, and dedication to master the basics."

Alma picked up the nib, placed it in Rick's hand, and carefully adjusted it until he held the nib correctly. With the nib on the left and his fingers supporting the shaft that was leaning slightly to the right, he was ready to continue his lesson.

It felt uncomfortable. Rick began to adjust to a more comfortable position before being corrected.

"Leave it there, Rick. Trust me."

Rick allowed Alma to reposition the nib. "Now, draw your line," she said.

Rick drew a solid, smooth, and clean line. The best to this point, but it was far from perfect. He was amazed at how effortlessly the ink flowed from the nib.

"Well, that would have been nice to know when I first walked in," Rick muttered.

"You weren't ready for it, Rick. You wouldn't have stayed with it. Now that you've spent a few hours struggling to find the perfect line, you're ready to accept a better way of doing things."

Rick knew she was right. He had spent most of his life doing things his way, even when others had tried to guide him. The lesson brought back a memory of kindergarten, when he was first taught the proper way to hold a pencil. It had hurt his fingers, so he'd adopted his own, more comfortable grip instead. His handwriting had suffered ever since.

After all these years, he hadn't bothered to correct it — what was the point? These days, he spent most of his time typing and rarely wrote anything by hand.

"What exactly are we talking about?" Rick asked, pausing to look up at Alma. "Are we talking about art or life?"

Alma smiled, a smile that seemed to hold a secret. "Couldn't it be one and the same? Seems to me there's an art to a life well lived."

Rick nodded. There were certainly those in the world whom he had met that seemed to have it all figured out.

Alma didn't give him time to finish his thought.

"Okay, stay with it. I'll be back in a while," Alma said.

"You're leaving?"

She just laughed, turned her back and waved playfully.

Over the course of several hours, Rick immersed himself in the art of drawing. He tirelessly explored different techniques in his quest for the perfect line. He meticulously crafted horizontal lines, vertical lines, and diagonal lines, each with their own unique lengths and widths, as if sculpting the very essence of his vision onto the canvas, though nothing ever seemed to match his exact vision.

He manipulated the weight of the lines with precision. With focus, he alternated between different types of pressure. With some, he left bold impressions on the surface. With others, he delicately applied a light touch, creating gentle strokes that seemed to dance gracefully on the page, so light that they were barely visible.

As time slipped away unnoticed, Rick's dedication didn't waver. The rumblings of hunger were drowned out by focus and determination to uncover the essence of the perfect line. He continued, until eventually, fatigue began to wear on his hand, the strain becoming increasingly unbearable. Despite the discomfort, Rick persisted.

Finally, the moment arrived when his hand could no longer endure the pain. With a mixture of satisfaction and exhaustion, Rick reluctantly set down the nib and tenderly massaged his tired hand, attempting to reprieve the ache.

"I give up. There's no such thing as a perfect line," he shouted looking up to the rafters in anger. His voice echoed through the warehouse studio.

From the corner of his eye, a faint glow rose from his sketch pad, the same way the paintings in the studio gave light. The light then quickly faded. Had he imagined it?

Desperate to re-create the light, Rick began scrawling line after line, but nothing happened. Rick thought back to what he had said just moments before.

"There's no such thing as perfection," he shouted again with certainty. He slammed his fists against the table in a fit of frustration.

Suddenly, every drop of ink he had painstakingly laid down in the hours before ignited with a steady, radiant glow — pulsing in rhythm with the realization settling deep within him. The lines, once ordinary and black, shimmered with a quiet hum, their glow shifting and deepening until the inky black bled into a vivid electric blue. The air itself seemed to vibrate, charged with meaning, as if understanding alone had awakened the lines and brought them to life.

"Ah, I see you found another truth."

Rick spun around to see El. He had on the same white lab coat covered in splatters of paint from the night before. Rick couldn't help but wonder if he always wore it, even away from the studio.

"What?"

"Congratulations, Rick, you've found another truth on this journey."

Rick was confused. What did he mean when he said that he had found another truth?

"Rick, have you ever heard something or been taught something that just felt right? Something that resonated deep down inside of you?"

"Sure I have," Rick said, trying to piece together the riddle of words.

"That's what happened here. The canvas can recognize truth. You said something that resonated with it. All great art resonates truth. That's why you can cry when you hear a song, get emotional when you watch a film, or feel something when you look at a canvas. We're able to connect with the emotions the artist places in it. It's the reason you get chills in a moment that confirms you're exactly where you need to be at that moment in your life."

Rick remembered the feeling he'd experienced when he walked through the doors that morning. When he felt bathed in the energy and electricity of the studio.

"There's no such thing as a perfect line. That's where the electric-blue glow came from?" Rick said again, as the sketch pad hummed with energy and gave off an even brighter glow. "That's the truth I discovered? That perfection doesn't exist? You had me sit here for hours in pursuit of a perfect line that you knew would never exist?"

El smiled a humble smile, apologetic. "I'm sorry, Rick. I couldn't just tell you that. That's not how it works here at Zivot Studio. You had to discover the meaning from your efforts and challenges. It's in our struggle that we most often find meaning.

"Besides, what is a perfect line, anyway? A straight, seemingly misplaced line can be so boring! The beauty lies in how it's used." His voice trailed off, accompanied by a soft laugh.

Rick was angry. He had wasted hours, and he still didn't really know why he was here.

"I know you're angry, Rick." El turned back, holding out his hands as if to say, "Get over it." "I didn't mean to trick you. Come on, follow me."

Reluctantly, Rick followed El to the far wall of the studio, where large military cabinets had been repurposed to store art supplies. It was clear this part of the studio didn't see much use. Rick noticed El's footprints ahead of him, the only marks in the fine layer of dust covering the floor.

El positioned a small step stool in front of a cabinet and reached up to retrieve a single canvas propped against the wall. Yellowed with age, the canvas was also coated in a thin layer of dust. Faint italic script across its surface read, "Kakve su ti misli, takav ti je život."

"What is that supposed to mean?" Rick asked, "I don't speak Russian."

"It's Croatian, Rick, not Russian. Not only is it in a language you don't speak, but it's on one of the smallest canvases here, tucked away where most would never look. People are too focused on the big canvases, the ones that are in your face, but this one canvas may be more powerful than anything else in this building."

El handed the canvas to Rick and reached for a large, clean, dry paint brush. He lightly swept the brush across the italicized words, clearing the dust. As he did, an electric-blue light illuminated the ink as the brush passed by and the words changed from "Kakve su ti misli, takav ti je život" to "What your thoughts are, such is your life."

"That's the problem, Rick. You're disappointed and frustrated with your life right now, like so many others. Most people are so consumed with chasing the perfect version of their lives that they fall apart when unexpected turns come their way. The moment things deviate from their plan, they become upset and angry. They fail to see the good that already exists in their lives — or the opportunity to create something entirely new. But that's not what Zivot is about."

"Zivot?" Rick asked. He had heard the studio name but never thought to ask what it meant.

"Life, Rick. Zivot is life, and no matter what social media might show or say, the ideal life doesn't exist. It's a myth — a false sense of control. The reality is, we have very little control over most things in life. A meaningful life is less about following a flawless plan and more about creating opportunities and adapting as needed. The masterpieces we admire aren't made of flawless lines. They're built layer by layer, with overlapping strokes that form intricate designs. The greatest artists don't aim for flawlessness — they focus on choosing the right stroke for the moment."

In that instant, something shifted for Rick. He said aloud, "Everyone comes here with a blank canvas. Only when we pick up the pen do we begin to create something meaningful — and it's never about perfection. It's the irregularities, the unexpected turns, that make each piece distinctive and give it character."

"That's right, Rick. Each life has the potential to become a masterpiece, but it always begins with I. When we are born, we hopefully have nurturing parents to teach us. Sometimes we don't, but regardless, life begins with I. I learned to eat. I learned to crawl. I learned to walk. It's my life and I must create it, regardless of the circumstances. No one can take the pen for us. That doesn't mean the art of life revolves around I, but it always begins with I. You learn later that it is the interaction with others that adds true beauty, color, and depth to our work. But I must live my life."

Then, in that moment, Rick realized why the image on the studio door that morning had displayed his flawed, ink-blotted attempt at a line. As he looked across the room, Rick discovered that El had saved the first rough line that Rick had attempted the night before. El had framed it, turned it vertically, and it clearly read as an italicized i. It was imperfect and unfinished, just like Rick, but it was worthy of display.

Rick turned to El, "I had to be the one to open the door to the studio today and choose to learn!"

"Ah!" El exclaimed, "That's amazing, Rick. Without any help, you just discovered the line of accountability. You owned your actions! Not many discover that in this life."

As Rick returned his gaze from the framed image to El, his mentor simply smiled, a glimmer of mischief in his wild eyes. The soft hum of the illuminated canvases grew louder, filling the studio with an almost tangible energy.

"El was right," Rick thought to himself. The imperfect i glowed brightly, its light casting intricate shadows across the room, tying together every stroke, every choice, every lesson.

El broke the silence. "I learned something important early in my life, while living in Japan. I'll have to tell you the whole story sometime.

"Let's just say Japan — like its people — has a way of teaching you things quietly, through moments that don't seem important until later.

"That's where I discovered wabi-sabi...

"Wabi-sabi is a Japanese concept — it teaches us to embrace the beauty in what's unfinished, Rick. It reminds us that flaws aren't failures; they're part of the story. They're what make the art and the artist real.

"But understanding it isn't enough. To truly honor it, you have to act. You have to create."

Rick felt the weight of the nib in his hand. The hum of the room seemed to tease him. "You are ready for the next line, Rick." El whispered, his voice almost lost in the vibration of the room. "Are you ready to find it?"

As El posed the question, Rick's phone buzzed.

He glanced at the screen. Chase Mercer.

The name hit like an old echo — familiar but jarring. A voice from another life. Chase was the walking cliché of a finance bro — the kind of guy Rick had spent his career both envying and despising.

Rick had been on that track once. Until he lost his wife.

After that, something shifted. Instead of pushing forward, he stalled. Maybe he told himself he was choosing something better, but the truth was, he'd just been coasting. Maybe that's why they let him go.

Either way, Chase Mercer was the last person he expected to call.

"Rick, are you ready?" El repeated.

Rick didn't answer. Not El. Not Chase. Not even his own thoughts.

He pocketed his phone and walked out, unsure if he was leaving behind an awakening — or retreating to a familiar past.

CHAPTER 5

TIMELINES

It had been weeks since Rick had set foot in the studio — weeks of avoiding the hum of the canvases, El's lessons, and the truth he wasn't ready to accept: that perfection didn't exist.

Even after everything, he still clung to the idea that it might. He clawed desperately to recover the life he once had.

Instead of leaning into the present, he retreated to the familiar comfort of numbers, outcomes, and someone who had never stopped chasing the next big win. He ignored the missed calls and texts from El, but eventually answered the ones from Chase Mercer — the finance bro from a past life he thought he'd outgrown.

Those phone calls with Chase led him to this very moment.

Now, seated across from his former colleague in a local deli — a place someone like Chase would never be caught dead in — Rick stirred the ice in his water, half-listening as the man rattled on about deals, market shifts, crypto, the usual.

Living up to his name, Chase was always chasing the next big opportunity. This time, it wasn't just the boutique venture capital firm he worked with — it was a struggling fintech startup they'd recently backed. For the better part of an hour, he'd been trying to rope Rick in, insisting the company had solid fundamentals and just needed the right leadership to turn things around. He thought Rick was right for the job.

But to Rick, it felt like pity. Or worse — an excuse for Chase to flaunt his success and remind Rick of his own shortcomings.

"Come on, Rick, the numbers are good. You can see that. What was the old saying you had?" Chase tapped the side of his glass of ice water, a smug grin tugging at the corner of his mouth. "Trust the math, not the mood, right?"

Rick knew he was right. On paper, it looked like a solid deal.

But he also knew he was restless — ready to get back to work — and for the first time in a long while, he questioned whether he was seeing the numbers clearly.

Was it a smart move, or just a lifeline disguised as logic? Desperation had a way of dressing up as opportunity. And that made it dangerous.

Rick had sent over his résumé when Chase first called, barely thinking twice — never actually expecting a response. And yet, here he was, sitting across from Chase Mercer of all people, wondering how his life had veered so far off course that this conversation was even possible.

Rick glanced out the window, watching the steady stream of people, wondering where they were off to — what their lives looked like, how much of them still felt intact.

Chase, reading the silence, leaned forward. "Look, man, this isn't pity. I actually give a damn," he said, dropping the smirk for the first time that afternoon. "Dude, what happened to you? We were on top of the world. I know Bridgette's passing hit you hard, but I never thought I'd see you like this."

Rick stiffened. He didn't want to revisit the past, but Chase had pulled him into it anyway.

"When I lost Bridgette, everything changed," Rick said, voice flat, like stating a fact.

Chase exhaled, shaking his head. "That's why we need to get you back in the game."

He slapped the table — a sharp, matter-of-fact punctuation mark — startling the waitress as she placed the check between them.

Rick barely looked at it. Instinct took over. An old reflex from a life where money was never a concern. He slid his card into the reader, anxious to put the conversation behind him.

Declined.

His stomach clenched. He flipped the card over, tried again.

Declined.

A hollow feeling crawled into his chest. He'd forgotten — no steady paychecks, no automatic transfers.

For a second, he almost wished for the kind of magic he'd glimpsed in the studio — something to rescue him from the moment. But the world outside the studio wasn't built on that.

Chase let out a low chuckle, shaking his head and releasing a string of expletives. "Guess the artist lifestyle doesn't cover lunch."

Rick had that coming.

He'd made the mistake of sharing the strange occurrences — the magical canvas, the mysterious studio — things he barely understood himself. He should have known better.

Chase wasn't the type to let something fanciful like that go. The only magic he believed in was the enchanting glow of diamond cufflinks and compounding interest.

Before Rick could reach for another card, Chase was already flashing his card — sleek, black, titanium. Another reminder of Rick's failure. Effortless. He tapped it against the reader with a smirk, his Rolex peeking from beneath his cuff like a silent reminder of who won this round.

Rick exhaled slowly.

"See?" Chase leaned back, stretching his arms, victory settling in. "That's why you can't just disappear. The world doesn't wait. You're either playing the game, or you're watching from the sidelines."

Rick didn't answer. He wasn't even bothered by Chase's smugness anymore.

Instead, his focus was on the sound of a soft, feminine, paint-splattered hand tapping on the window next to him.

Rick turned in the direction of the sound. It was Alma.

She grinned through the window, her enthusiasm contagious. For a moment, he felt like a high school kid — caught off guard, giddy with the surprise.

His mindset shifted.

He pushed back his chair and stood. "Hey, Chase, great catching up. You've got my résumé." He paused for just a beat, eyes steady. "If there's a fit, I'd love to hear more."

He offered a quick nod. "I've got to run."

Chase barely had time to react before Rick was already heading for the door, smiling widely at Alma.

Putting two and two together, Chase smirked. "I see what this art fascination is really about," he called out smugly.

Rick didn't bother looking back.

He had already crossed the line — from Chase's world to the welcoming smile of Alma.

Before he could process it, she wrapped him in an unexpected hug. They barely knew each other, but from her playful grin, he could tell the gesture wasn't unusual. That's just who she was.

"What are you doing here?" he asked, genuinely surprised.

"Would you believe it was a coincidence?" Alma teased, her eyes glinting.

Rick wasn't sure that it was.

Before he had a chance to reply, she threw another question at him. "Why haven't you been back to the studio?"

Rick's excitement momentarily dulled. He glanced upward, stalling. "I don't know. Not sure that's my thing. I'm not much for art."

When he looked back, Alma was already moving. The crosswalk signal had changed and she stepped off the curb.

Rick hurried to catch up. He always seemed to be chasing her.

"Really, Rick?" Her eyes crinkled in disbelief as she glanced over her shoulder.

They continued walking.

"What do you mean by that?" He asked.

"I think you're afraid," Alma's accusation was direct.

"I'm not afraid. I just don't see the point. Lines, art — it's not really my thing."

Alma tugged at his hand, motioning toward a nearby bench. "Maybe that's the problem. Have you given it a chance?"

They sat on the bench, and Alma continued. "El wants you to come back. To try again."

"Just El?" Rick asked, voice dipping into flirtation.

She rolled her eyes. "Well, we both do."

Rick shrugged. "I don't know. I've got to find work."

"It doesn't have to be a full-time thing," she said, softening the invitation. "There's a community art class tonight. El's running it. He wants you to come — and bring your canvas."

Rick's thoughts twisted. Experimenting on his own was one thing. A classroom setting? That was different.

"I'll think about it. But why does it matter to you so much?"

Alma paused, her expression softening. "Because I know what these lessons can do for you, Rick. I know it doesn't come naturally, but you just need a little faith. That's what I had to do — and I've never looked back."

Rick raised an eyebrow. "So you actually think there's something to all this? That a line holds power?"

She smiled. "Not at first. But the longer I stayed, the more I felt like I was led to the studio. It changed my life."

Rick exhaled. "You think an art class is going to change my life?"

Now, Alma's tone shifted. More serious. More certain. "There's only one way to find out, and it's not going to happen sitting on this bench."

She stood, then crouched down and picked up a small stone from the pavement, turning it between her fingers.

"You ever think about time, Rick?" Alma asked.

Rick smirked. "More than I'd like to." It was true — with his dwindling bank account, he couldn't help but wonder how much time he had.

She tossed the stone up, catching it with ease. "Most people only think about time one way — the kind that moves forward, second by second, paycheck to paycheck. That's chronos." She nodded toward the traffic, the blinking crosswalk, a man checking his watch. "Measured time. Schedules. Deadlines."

Rick exhaled. "Yeah, I know the type."

Alma, still crouching, picked up a jagged stone and pressed it to the pavement. With slow, deliberate motion, she scraped it across the concrete, left to right, etching a rough, unmistakable line.

"Chronos," she said, as the line grew longer. "It's how most people live — step by step, day by day. They don't even realize it's happening. Everything happens on a linear timeline."

She paused, then added one circled point at the start of the line. "Birth," she said simply.

She added another circle at the end of the line. "Death."

Rick leaned in, watching her map out other moments of modern life as it's usually lived.

"But kairos..." she glanced up. "Kairos is different. It shows up here," she tapped a spot between the marks, "or maybe here," she tapped another point, "and it changes everything."

Rick stared at the etch in the concrete. It didn't look like much. But somehow, it captured his attention.

"Kairos is Greek for 'the right time,'" she said, not looking up. "The kind you don't plan for but have to recognize."

"Kairos isn't about how long you've been walking. It's about recognizing the moment you're supposed to turn another direction. It's the moment when opportunity presents itself."

Rick stared at Alma's line on the concrete. "Sounds like another way of saying 'luck.'"

Alma smiled, shaking her head. "Luck is blind. Kairos is about seeing — knowing when to step up, even if it wasn't in your plan." She straightened, brushing dust from her hands. "Like when you walked into that studio. Was that just coincidence?"

Rick shrugged. "Who knows?"

"Then why does it keep pulling at you?" She studied him for a moment. "Chronos is steady and consistent. It moves forward whether you do or not. But kairos? That's a door that won't stay open forever. It's a spark — brief, fleeting opportunity — waiting to be caught before the moment disappears. Opportunities of a lifetime don't live forever."

Rick rubbed his jaw, suddenly uncomfortable.

Alma held out the stone. "So tell me, Rick — are you just taking up time, or are you ready to make your mark? Are you ready to seize the opportunity life has given you?"

Rick didn't answer. He recalled a quote from Winston Churchill.

"To each there comes in their lifetime a special moment when they are figuratively tapped on the shoulder and offered the chance to do a very special thing, unique to them and fitted to their talents."

He had heard it once in a lecture hall, but it never hit this close and so hard.

"What a tragedy if that moment finds them unprepared or unqualified for that which could have been their finest hour."

Rick had never forgotten that lesson.

And now, standing at the edge of a choice he hadn't seen coming, he wondered — was this his moment?

Alma turned, walking toward the studio in the distance. "Chronos keeps moving," she called over her shoulder. "Kairos? You have to choose."

And in that moment, Rick understood.

Chronos gives us time to act. But when kairos comes along, time holds its breath and offers the opportunity of a lifetime. These moments rarely show up on a timeline. You have to capture them.

He stared at the line Alma had scratched on the pavement.

Then, making a choice, he stepped over it and headed home to retrieve the canvas before heading to the studio.

Behind him, a small crowd had gathered, drawn by the electric-blue glow now pulsing from the line Alma had carved into the pavement.

What had started as a simple scratch in the pavement — a rough, imperfect gesture — had become something more: a glowing invitation for others to challenge their timeline.

Pedestrians stood huddled around it, staring not just at the light, but also trying to understand the message it seemed to carry.

They had yet to discover the power of a line.

CHAPTER 6

UNLIMITED POTENTIAL

Rick hadn't planned on returning to the studio. Not today.

But Alma's words — "Chronos keeps moving. Kairos? You have to choose" — still echoed in his mind.

He had stood there, staring at the glowing line she scratched into the pavement, feeling something stir.
It wasn't pressure.
It wasn't even clarity.
It was possibility.
Now, standing just outside his apartment, he faced another line: the threshold between hesitation and action.

He stepped inside, grabbed the canvas, and without letting himself second-guess, turned toward the studio.

This time, he wasn't drifting. He wasn't reacting. He was choosing.

At the entrance to Zivot Studio, the familiar hum met him again. Canvases glowed. Voices murmured. But something was different — he was different. He had crossed a line.

At the long butcher-block tables, students were already seated. Some leaned forward, curious. Others slouched, guarded, skeptical.

Rick noticed the contrast. A few hours ago, he might not have cared. He might have been one of them.

A voice cut through the room: "I can't believe I'm even here. This better be worth my time."

Rick didn't flinch, but something in him did tighten. Was that how he'd sounded before? How many chances had he brushed off without realizing they were moments that mattered?

He didn't want to sit near that voice.

Instead, he found a spot near others who looked undecided but open — people on the edge of their own line. He set his canvas down.

This time, he wasn't just passing time; he was here to make his mark.

A part of him — just for a second — wondered if the canvas might look different; if something had shifted since he had finally chosen to bring it. But when he turned it over, it had transitioned back to the same solid black line that he first discovered.

Maybe it wasn't the canvas that needed to change.

At the front of the room, Alma was arranging supplies, speaking quietly with El. She glanced up, catching Rick's eye, a knowing smile tugging at the corner of her lips.

She had known he would come.

Beside her, El stood with a grin that couldn't stay contained. Where Alma carried quiet certainty, El carried enthusiasm that finally spilled over.

"Rick! Rick, my boy, come up here. I saved you a seat — bring your canvas!"

El's voice rang out, pulling him forward.

Startled, Rick looked up. El, in his signature paint-splattered lab coat, waved him forward, his unruly hair punctuating the gesture like exclamation points. At the front, a single empty stool awaited at a table near El, where three students already sat, their eyes now on Rick.

Reluctantly, Rick made his way to the front, feeling the weight of an entire room's eyes on him. He placed the canvas on the table and took the seat El had saved.

As Rick settled in, El's energy filled the room, commanding attention.

"Welcome to a space where curiosity unlocks discovery!" he said, pacing in front of the room. "Some of you are here because you want to be. Some of you..." he paused, scanning the room, grinning, "are here because someone else thought you should be here."

A few chuckles. A few groans.

El smirked. "That's right. Some of you are here because you're working toward your GED or continuing education credits. Some because your therapist recommended it — said it might help with stress or self-expression. And some of you..." he scanned the room, his grin widening, "are taking this as part of your recovery journey."

The room went still for a beat.

El's voice softened, but his conviction stayed strong. "Whatever the reason, all are welcome."

Rick glanced around. Now he saw it. Some students were leaning in, eager. Others sat stiffly, arms crossed, waiting for the clock to run out.

El let the moment breathe before continuing.

"But here's what I want you to think about," he said, clasping his hands. "What if it doesn't matter why you came? What if the only thing that matters is what you do now that you're here?"

A few heads lifted. Others stayed skeptical. But Rick felt something shift.

El's gaze moved across the room. "Like art, even familiar lessons reveal something new, depending on how you view them."

Rick smirked at El's audacity.

El's expression turned serious again. "Here, every question is a key, and every answer holds the spark of another question. Together, we'll push boundaries and uncover something unexpected. Let's make the most of this journey."

Then, turning to Rick, El smiled. "Let's begin by examining a new canvas. Rick, come on up. Bring your canvas — you can place it on the easel."

Come up? Rick froze. Was El serious? He wasn't an artist. He wanted to run.

"Come on," El urged again.

Reluctantly, Rick stood. He lifted the canvas and walked to the front of the room, where he placed the canvas on the easel. The thick black line was now on display for all to view.

Rick started to make his way back to his seat.

"Wait, Rick," El stopped him, "stay here. Teach us. I need you to teach us."

Rick froze, his feet rooted to the spot in front of the classroom. A nervous laugh escaped his lips, shaky and uncertain.

"You want me to teach?" His voice wavered. His hands fidgeted at his sides before he quickly turned to the canvas, locking eyes on the single black line as if searching for an escape.

A few students chuckled. "Yeah, teach us, Picasso," someone muttered from the back.

A smattering of laughs followed.

Rick's stomach tightened.

Someone exaggerated a yawn. Another gave a slow, mocking clap. Rick clenched his jaw, suddenly aware of how exposed he felt. He didn't belong here. He wasn't an artist. He had no business standing in front of this class.

He studied the canvas, its focal point the single, bold black line stretching across the center. It stared back at him, silent — offering nothing.

To help him, El spoke up, motioning to the canvas and the line. "Tell us about it, Rick. What is it?"

Rick swallowed hard. "I guess I don't know. A line?" His words came out flat, hollow. With all the discussion about lines, he assumed that was the answer El was looking for.

Those forced to be there mocked with laughter.

El studied him for a moment. Rick wasn't sure if El's look conveyed disappointment or something else.

Then El leaned in. "You're better than that, Rick. You're an artist."

The laughter continued.

"Oh, get over yourselves," a voice cut through the laughter — sharp, composed, undeniably British.

The room fell silent.

Rick turned toward the voice and saw a stranger stepping forward.

She carried an effortless confidence, poised but unfazed, her gaze steady as she scanned the room. Who was she? Her accent alone demanded attention.

She arched an eyebrow. "Honestly, do none of you remember coming up here?"

A few students shifted. No one answered.

She sighed. "That's what I thought. But go on, do keep heckling him. It's always easier to sit in the back than to stand up and create."

El grinned but stayed quiet, letting her take control, knowing the monumental breakthrough this moment was in this woman's own journey.

She turned to Rick, her expression softening. "Don't mind them," she said, amusement flickering in her voice. "Some of us are still recovering cynics." She looked at the students with disdain.

Rick exhaled and nervously smiled as his clenched hands loosened slightly.

The older woman leaned back, arms crossed, as if she had once stood exactly where he was now.

Then she turned back to the class. "Come on then, let's help him. You lot are so eager to criticize — so tell me, what do you see?"

Her words hung in the air — a challenge, but not unkind.

She gestured toward the room. "Well? What do you see? No need to raise your hand, just call it out."

There was a moment of silence and then the first brave soul spoke up.

"It divides two spaces. It's suggesting limits."

Another member of the class followed.

"It's a basic geometric element. It's fundamental to creating shapes and structures."

"Good," the lady nodded, acknowledging the two comments. "What else? Look beyond the obvious, what do you see? View the canvas as an artist."

The class began to rattle off thought after thought, unique variations of what they saw. An endless list of possibilities followed.

A line could represent a path, a journey, a boundary, a horizon, a connection, a bridge, a direction, an edge, a limit, a guide, a thread, a link, a communication channel, an axis, an outline, a stroke of genius.

Rick was surprised by the number of answers, many he had not yet even considered. He was immediately taken back to one of El's first lessons about the line of interpretation.

"Fantastic!" El exclaimed, jumping back into the role of the instructor. "Keep going, let the universe feed you," he said, almost tauntingly. El met her eyes and gave a subtle nod to the British woman who had stepped in for Rick—a quiet recognition of her timing, authority, and the journey that had led her here.

The class continued, "It's a line of demarcation, a trajectory, a signpost on a map, a ray, a stitch in sewing, a hyphen, a boundary in sports, a route in a network, a beam in construction, a streak in the sky, a filament, a stage."

El held his hands to his chest like a proud father. He savored every remark. "We could probably go on like this for hours. But it's Rick's turn. Okay, Rick." El turned back to his new apprentice. "A lot of ideas are out there. But this is your canvas, so what is it?"

Rick considered the suggestions that the group had given. Their varying views caused Rick to re-examine his own. He had never given that much consideration to something so simple. His biased left brain only saw one thing, but his right brain, the center for creativity, was beginning to awaken. He was seeing the world in a different light. He considered how he was viewing his current experience, the one that devastated his career. Was the job a loss? Or was it something different?

He looked again at the line on the canvas, contemplating its purpose, then the answer came to him. It was the one thing that he needed more than anything else right now.

Rick looked confidently at El and then at the rest of the audience, then he stated with an emphatic tone, "It's a starting line." He hadn't spoken so confidently in a very long time.

El nodded approvingly. "With all the possibilities that are out there, I think I might like that one the best. A starting line is noble. It provides a great place to create from and one I think we all can use on occasion. You may sit down now, Rick."

Rick returned to his seat as the class sat in quiet contemplation.

El continued, "There are a number of things we can learn here. I think the first is the most obvious. Depending on our experiences, what we need, and what we expect, a line can literally be anything we want it to be. Like life, we all see the line just a little differently."

The room fell into a hushed stillness, every eye fixed on El as if drawn by an invisible force. His movements were methodical, his voice carrying an intensity that seemed to command attention. Rick couldn't look away; it was as though El had tapped into something beyond charisma — something ethereal, commanding the room in a way Rick had rarely seen before.

"Now, I know this next question is a dangerous one. Do we have any Yankees fans with us?" Most of the class let out a whoop or applauded. "How about the Mets?" Boos filled the room, except for a few indignant Mets fans.

"Okay, how about Coke or Pepsi? Which is better?" The room erupted into a chaotic den of opinions.

Rick smiled as he immediately saw what El was doing.

El motioned for the sound to quiet down. Slowly, the rumblings calmed.

As the room settled into the discussion, El began his next lesson.

"Wow, I'm glad I didn't ask about politics." A few in the class laughed. "Isn't it interesting how many opinions a question can provoke? Think about all the interpretations we got just discussing a line. All answers were in some way influenced by everyone's life experiences."

The class pondered.

"So who is right?" El posed the question.

There were fewer interruptions, until one spoke up. "I guess we all are!"

Someone else followed up with, "Maybe we're all wrong."

The room began to chatter with opinion.

"Interesting," El motioned for the room to calm down. "The older I get, the more I realize that there are very few correct answers, but there are many opinions because we all have different experiences. There are very few absolute truths, but there is one truth I want you to focus on — you get to assign meaning to every line on your canvas."

There were a few nods in the class.

"We're going to talk much more about art, but while I have you here, I want you to consider, just for a moment, the art of life." El's voice, though steady, cut off midsentence as a sudden, violent cough overtook him. It wasn't a clearing of the throat — it was deep, ragged, and unrelenting.

"I'm sorry!" He staggered, one hand clutching his chest, the other fumbling for the nearest stool. His fingers gripped the edge just in time to steady himself.

The room went still as he gathered his composure.

"I need everyone to pay attention — this is important," he said firmly, his eyes narrowing as he noticed two students whispering in the back of the room. "Listen up," he repeated, his impatience cutting through the quiet. "There are two lines we're about to discuss, and everyone needs to understand them. I won't ask you to master them yet. That will come with time. For now, you just need to grasp their significance. Your success in using them is dependent on your interpretations."

El paused, wiping the perspiration from his brow. The beads of sweat caught the light, underscoring the gravity of the moment. "Throughout our time together, you've heard me say that every line has a start and a stop. But," he continued, "I must confess — that's only partially true. There is one line that breaks those rules. Can anyone tell me what it is?"

The room remained silent, the students' faces attentive and expectant.

"The timeline," El said emphatically, his voice resonating with conviction. "It's the exception. Unlike other lines, a timeline isn't bound by a single start or stop. It's made up of countless beginnings and endings, each one shaping the next. Rick already shared his starting line, but that's just one piece of the puzzle. Too often, we see the finish line as a conclusion, but I've learned that every end is also a new beginning.

"A timeline is more than just a measure of time — it's a map of our experiences, relationships, actions, and impact. Its segments may vary in length, and when one ends, it doesn't mean we've failed. It simply marks a transition. But let me remind you, every timeline will eventually reach its final end. Use your time wisely."

He straightened himself, catching his balance, and his tone shifted, becoming even more resolute. "That brings us to our next lesson."

El made his way to a nearby whiteboard. Taking a black marker, he wrote the following in the upper left-hand corner of the whiteboard

Live Intentionally. No Excuses.

Rick watched as the class took notes and captured El's definition in the margins of their sketch pads.

"Pay close attention," El said, curling his fingers into a fist for emphasis. "That is the line of intention!"

El cleared his throat. "When we are deliberate with how we use the limited supply of ink we have been given in this life, we can live intentionally with no excuses. The best way for us to do that is to ensure that as we live, we also love, learn, and lead intentionally. No excuses.

"We've just seen that there are hundreds of ways to interpret a line. There are probably millions of ways to interpret life. So why not do ourselves a favor? Let's interpret the marks on our canvas, good or bad, in such a way that benefits us. We can do that if we are intentional. Remember, what a 'LINE' is — a reminder to Live Intentionally. No Excuses."

His eyes sharpened with intent as he stepped forward, marker in hand. With deliberate strokes, he re-created Rick's line on the whiteboard — bold, thick, and unmistakably deliberate.

"The line of intention brings clarity to our work and purpose to our actions. In the end, our thoughtful selections and prioritization of what we place on our canvas should create a sense of balance," El said.

"Balance," he continued, his tone reflective, "is about creating stability. As humans, we're naturally drawn to it. We crave consistency, and when life is out of balance, it feels chaotic and unsettling. The same is true for art — if something is off balance, we sense it immediately. Our intentional response can help us to restore balance."

With care, El sketched a triangle below the far-left side of the line he had just drawn — a stark symbol of imbalance. He followed quickly with a large square, positioned above the line's far-right end. Though the line remained straight, the image illustrated a dissonance, an unsettling lack of harmony.

"Notice how the arrangement of these shapes creates imbalance. Despite the straightness of the line, the composition feels off."

The room fell silent as the students absorbed the simplicity and depth of his demonstration.

"With just a few adjustments, balance can be restored," El continued, erasing the triangle. Carefully, he redrew it, centering it perfectly below the line, then added a square above the line to the far left. "A little symmetry brings everything back into harmony."

Rick sat up. It was against his nature, but he spoke his mind out loud. "I don't think that's true, El. At least not in life." He paused. "People want to treat balance like a neat equation — split everything evenly, and life just works. But that's not how time operates."

He let it sit.

"You get twenty-four hours. Take out sleep, and you have sixteen. Now we're expected to fit in work, family, health, growth — equally? You can't. Something always takes priority."

He scanned the room. Some nodded. Others waited.

"Balance assumes everything gets equal weight. But life doesn't split our time evenly. Some seasons demand more from work, others from family, and sometimes from yourself. Try to force balance, and you'll break."

Rick exhaled. "Balance is an illusion. Harmony is the goal. It's about adjusting, shifting with life, knowing when to lean in and when to let go — without losing yourself in the process."

Silence filled the room, wondering how El would react.

Some leaned in. Others frowned, thinking.

El stood there for a moment, contemplative — then his face broke into a wide grin. A deep, raucous laugh erupted from his soul, followed by a slow, deliberate applause.

"And that! That right there is the beauty of a working studio. The greatest lessons don't come from me — they come from the work itself."

He beamed, pride gleaming in his eyes as he took in his returning pupil's discovery.

In that moment, the image emitted an electric-blue glow, emphasizing the need for harmony. The room fell silent, each person lost in thought and deeply connected through the lesson. Rick felt a shift within himself.

"That's a great place to end things."

As the class ended, most of the students wandered off. Very few paid attention to the physical condition that they left the studio in. There was paper on the floor, chairs were askew, and ink bottles were left opened on the tables. Rick stayed around to help. He didn't have anywhere in particular to be. And he enjoyed his time in the studio. He had been taught to always leave things better than he found them. Besides, he had questions.

Once the chores were done and the studio was in good repair, El and Rick found themselves alone in the studio. The lessons from the night's activities still lingered in the air, and they both savored the tranquility that followed the bustling hours.

Rick dwelled on the things he had learned. He was beginning to appreciate the power of a line, and even more, the artistic approach to life taken by his friend. As he glanced at the colorful masterpieces adorning the walls, he recognized that each stroke carried a story, a glimpse into the soul of its creator. It was a reminder that within each person lies a world of untapped expression waiting to be discovered and shared. But there was something that stood out to Rick, something in stark contrast to what he had just been taught.

"What is it, Rick? What do you want to ask me?" El could sense a question in Rick's demeanor.

"You talked about rules — things every creation is supposed to follow, like balance. But looking around, a lot of these pieces break those rules."

Rick panned the room gesturing with his hands to point out the nuances to El.

El only smiled. "Rick, the world is full of rules. Many of them serve a great purpose."

Rick nodded in agreement.

"Imagine what would happen if you drove the wrong way on a one-way road. What would happen?" El asked, trying to reinforce the point.

Rick contemplated the potential dangers.

El leaned against a table, his voice steady and measured. "Laws exist to keep us safe, to provide order. But then there are opinions — rules people believe you must follow to live a happy life. Some of those opinions are helpful, and others... not so much."

He gestured toward Rick, his expression thoughtful. "Imagine if someone decided it was illegal to make anything other than vanilla ice cream. But you don't like vanilla — you like Rocky Road. That kind of rule would be pointless, grounded in someone else's opinion, not universal truth."

El paused, letting the words settle, his eyes scanning the room as if searching for connection. "The challenge," he said, softer now, "is learning to recognize which rules keep you safe and which ones hold you back."

"What's your point?" Rick asked, his tone edged with curiosity.

El smiled knowingly. "Some rules exist to protect us, to ensure safety and well-being. But then there are others — guidelines, really. Those are the ones you need to question and explore." He paused, gesturing subtly to the canvas. "Many incredible, well-respected artists became legends by breaking the rules of art. But before they could break them, they had to learn them. That's why we teach the fundamentals — to give new students a foundation. Once you've gained more experience, you'll start to see which rules are unshakable and which are meant to be bent — or even broken."

Looking around the room at the works of art, it began to make more sense. Rick saw many great works that generally followed the rules he had just been taught, but they also carried a sense of the creator and their own signature twist.

As if to put an exclamation mark on the conversation, El leaned in close and pulled up the sleeve of his lab coat to reveal the outline of a bold- lettered tattoo. It was a single line of text that ran the length of his outer forearm, directly over the bone, it read:

"Learn the rules like a pro, so you can break them like an artist."
– Pablo Picasso

The quote was accented by the illustration of a small butterfly emerging from its cocoon. The art clearly symbolized the line of adaptation embraced by the caterpillar who refused to accept its prior status and instead chose to adapt to a future state.

Rick studied El's tattoo, its meaning striking him deeply. His assumptions about life had been flawed. It was a reminder that life, like art, demanded intention and courage to break from the expected. He could stop reacting to his circumstances and shape them for his benefit.

He realized he had the power to define his experiences — not by following someone else's rules, but by creating his own. For too long, he'd moved through life without a plan, letting emotions and routine dictate his days. That approach wasn't going to work anymore.

Change would mean doing things differently, stepping away from old habits, and even challenging the expectations of others. Growth would require risk, courage, and willingness to innovate.

As he stood there, Rick felt ready. This was the starting line of a new canvas, and he was determined to make it his own.

CHAPTER 7

BAMBOO

Two weeks later, on a quiet morning, the memory of the community art class replayed in Rick's mind.

He had made his choice. Declared it publicly, even. But somewhere between resolution and reality, doubt slipped back in.

Rick's emotions had swung hard since he'd marked the canvas as his starting line — a public declaration of a fresh start. He'd doubled down after learning about El's tattoo. But the initial thrill had faded. Reality crept in: no job prospects, no clear path — just fear, anxiety, and the slow pull of doubt.

More than anything, Rick was growing frustrated with himself. He had every intention of embracing El's lessons, but time after time, he slipped back into old patterns.

And the canvas seemed to sense it. It had changed again.

Rick stared at it from the sofa, tired and confused. The new image wasn't his, nothing he'd drawn.

But the shape on the canvas held his gaze.

It hovered just above the black line he'd originally drawn. Was it a goal post? Or maybe a squared-off capital "H," but not one he recognized.

The crossbar sat high, stretched past the columns like arms reaching out. It was clean. Solid. Open.

A structure meant to be passed through.

Rick didn't know what it meant, but it felt like an invitation.

Its symmetry and precision reminded Rick more of a Japanese character than anything from the American alphabet.

Unable to identify the image, Rick pushed the memory to the recesses of his mind, tucking it away until he could speak to El. The uncertainty gnawed at him, but he hoped El might have answers — or at least provide the support Rick hadn't found elsewhere. Though he didn't feel like going to Zivot, he knew he needed to. He couldn't shake the funk he was in, and something told him El might be the only one who could help pull him out of it.

By the time he reached the studio, the weight of his emotions still pressed heavily on him. His shoulders slumped under its invisible burden, and his chest felt constricted, as though it bore the weight of his doubts and frustrations. He paused at the door, staring at the faint letters painted on the matte-gray surface — Zivot Studio. The words seemed to shimmer faintly in the light, inviting yet somehow daunting.

Taking a deep breath, Rick stepped inside. The familiar scents grounded him slightly but not enough to dispel the heaviness he felt. The studio was alive, with its scattered works in progress and faint energy humming in the air, but Rick felt disconnected from it. His gaze drifted to the large table in the center of the room, where El was hunched over a piece of art. His normally steady hand seemed to gently shake.

El glanced up, his eyes immediately narrowing with concern. "Rick," he said, his voice steady but soft. "You look like you've been carrying the world on your back."

Rick managed a weak smile. "It feels like it."

El set his tools aside and straightened, motioning for Rick to sit. "Then let's talk. Hopefully, the studio has some answers." El coughed softly into his fist, his voice was hoarse.

There was sincerity in his voice.

The new apprentice sat in contemplative silence for a moment. "Uh, I don't know exactly how to describe it, El. My mind is like a seesaw of emotions. One minute I'm excited, thinking this is a new beginning, an opportunity to start over; and the next, I feel like a complete and utter failure. I seem to question everything I've learned on this journey. Just when I thought I was beginning to discover my purpose, I get hit with this overwhelming doubt."

Rick paused. "I feel like I'm failing."

His voice barely rose above a whisper. He looked away from El, his eyes landing on the canvas now hanging prominently on the wall — a remnant from an earlier lesson.

The words read, "Kakve su ti misli, takav ti je život" — he recalled the meaning: "What your thoughts are, such is your life."

The script was clean and bold. The canvas had been dusted off and hung with care. It gleamed with purpose, a silent reminder of the studio's deeper truths — and of how far Rick felt from them now.

But in that moment, the words felt less like guidance and more like a provocation — taunting him. Daring him to rise above his feelings. Reminding him that he was, whether he liked it or not, shaping his own reality.

El gave an understanding smile. He had been there. El stretched out his arms to offer a reassuring hug. Rick wasn't a hugger. He wasn't emotional, at least he hadn't been, but El's hug was a welcome gesture. It was as authentic as the eccentric artist himself.

"I think I know what is happening, Rick."

"You do?" Rick believed him, but asked almost out of habit.

"Keep in mind, these lessons are all very new to you. What did the canvas show you this morning?" El's eyebrows lifted, his curiosity evident.

Of course, El would know. The connection between the studio and the canvas in his apartment was undeniable. With a reflective breath,

Rick began to describe the strange "H-like" image that had appeared earlier that morning.

Before Rick finished, El had taken out his cellphone and pulled up an image from a website. Knowingly, he smiled and asked, "Is this what you saw?"

On the screen was a photo of a traditional Japanese gate framed by ancient cedar and camphor trees — an unmistakable, three-dimensional match to the image on the canvas from earlier that day, down to the smallest detail.

Rick nodded in the affirmative, "Yes, that's it. What is it, El?"

El smiled — not out of joy, but remembrance. "That place means a lot to me from time in the military, Rick. It was painful, but also profound... have you ever heard of the Ise Grand Shrine in Japan?"

"No." Rick stood confused, and a bit upset. "Never heard of it. Why would that show up on my canvas if I've never seen it?"

El shrugged, "Maybe it was drawn for you? Synchronicities are very real, Rick."

Whether El didn't see the look of doubt on Rick's face, or he chose to ignore it, he continued. "I was stationed in Japan for a while. The Ise Grand Shrine is very special to the people and has deep meaning. Based on what you have told me, I'd suggest embracing its meaning in your life."

Rick just listened, never pushing back. "What do you mean?"

"The Ise Grand Shrine is a unique place, unlike any I'm aware of. It follows a tradition that goes back more than thirteen hundred years. The concept is such a contrast to the world we live in. Society says, 'Accept me just the way I am and don't ask me to change,' but the shrine is different. They rebuild the temple every twenty years. It's a statement of renewal, improvement, and commitment to embrace change. Did you ever hear the term Kaizen during your MBA program, Rick?"

"Sure, I have," Rick acknowledged. He remembered the term being popularized in the book *The Toyota Way*. He had read it many times. "It's a philosophy for continuous improvement."

"Good," El confirmed. "That's very applicable here. This temple embraces the essence of Kaizen, the principle of continuous improvement, reminding us that nothing in life is permanent. It's about reinvention. Every two decades, the shrine is completely rebuilt. The people believe in preserving tradition and keeping both the spiritual and physical aspects of life pure."

Rick looked bewildered. "They just tear it down?"

"That's right, they tear it down and rebuild it from scratch. The craftsmen use sacred Japanese cypress trees and painstakingly rebuild the temple. But what's truly remarkable is they leave the old foundation intact, serving as a silent witness to the passage of time."

"What does that have to do with me, El?" Rick hadn't fully grasped the concept.

"What you saw on the canvas, Rick, was a Japanese torii — a gateway. It's a symbol of transition, a threshold that requires anyone who passes through to do so willingly, embracing the possibility of change and reinvention.

"Remember when you named your line a starting line? The thing about starting lines is it only matters if you cross it. The same is true of a gate, the door to Zivot Studio, or any new beginning: You have to choose to move through it. No one else can take that step for you."

Rick was beginning to understand, "Then why is it so difficult, almost painful for me right now?"

"The truth is, you're straddling the starting line. You're caught somewhere between the past and the future. It's going to hurt, and it might even scar you for a bit. Change isn't easy; it can leave a mark. Do me a favor, Rick, and think about a bamboo plant. See it in your mind and describe it to me."

Rick closed his eyes, cleared his mind, and said, "It's incredibly strong, like wood, but it's hollow. It's tall and green and has a few leaves, but what's really noticeable are the horizontal lines on the trunk."

Rick opened his eyes to see El smile.

"That's right! In the studio, everything revolves around lines. It's fascinating how bamboo undergoes a similar process of reinventing itself, just like the Ise Grand Shrine." El glanced at Rick. "Did you know the giant bamboo plant can grow up to three and a half feet in a single day?

"Those lines we see on the bamboo? They're called nodes. Think of those lines as scars. They appear at periods of change, but in reality, they act as foundations for future growth. They provide the structure that will support the bamboo's continuous development.

"Just like picking up a new canvas, each line signifies closing a chapter and embarking on a new season of growth." El paused, watching Rick carefully, unsure if the meaning had truly settled in — if he recognized its significance in his own life.

"Are you a football guy, Rick?"

"Sure, I love football."

"Good. Then this might hit home. Think about that line on the bamboo plant as a line of scrimmage. Imagine this: The line of scrimmage is a battleground where the offense's drive for growth clashes with the defense's structural resistance. The defense knows growth is going to mean pain. The opposing sides test each other's strength and resolve. Growth demands progress, striving to push forward with force and determination, while resistance anchors the line, reinforcing stability. That's where the scarring takes place. Eventually though, the offense wins and the bamboo grows."

To emphasize the image, El clenched both hands into fists and pressed his knuckles together, illustrating a struggle of two forces pushing against each other in opposition. It was exactly how Rick's emotions felt.

"What I love about bamboo is its unwavering commitment to progress. Once those lines are drawn, a battle begins, but eventually, it moves forward. It never looks back. Instead, it reaches higher, embracing each new phase of growth and potential — until the next challenge comes, bringing with it another opportunity to grow."

El's voice softened. "Use the past as stepping stones. Let them lift you, not weigh you down."

A pause. Then: "Why don't you head home? Take the day to reflect on what you've learned and where you want to go from here. Watch your thoughts. Don't feed the negative ones, because when frustration hits — and it will — remember: Optimism is the artist of opportunity."

Rick glanced at El's arm — the butterfly tattoo. Surely, even that creature had questioned the pain of crawling from its cocoon before it took flight.

It made sense. Rick repeated the words, "Optimism is the artist of opportunity." As the words escaped his mouth, a palpable energy filled the room and began to glow with beautiful, electric-blue truth.

Rick, immersed in his thoughts and feeling overwhelmed yet hopeful, slowly turned away from El and thanked him for his time and advice. He knew he was right — Rick needed to decide whether he was ready to embrace the future or continue living in the past.

CHAPTER 8

A FILAMENT OF LIGHT

"Good morning! You're just in time for breakfast," Alma said, startling Rick as he walked through the doors of Zivot.

A small spread was laid out on one of the paint-splattered tables — juice, syrup, powdered sugar, and waffle batter — balanced precariously between brushes and sketch pads. El appeared to be spreading syrup evenly over a waffle with a fresh painter's brush, as if it were just another canvas. Rick gave him an odd look but didn't say anything. Somehow, it didn't surprise him.

It was his earliest start in the studio. Arriving just after sunrise, the building had a different feel about it and a different smell. Rick had been eager to start his day and continue his newly accepted apprenticeship. He had begun to recognize that this apprenticeship had more to do with life than art. For the first time in weeks, he felt like he was exactly where he was supposed to be.

"Good morning, Alma." The rich smell of oil paint and linseed oil, though fainter than the night before, was masked by the hearty aroma of bacon and toasted vanilla. A few weeks ago, Rick hadn't even heard of linseed oil, but now he recognized it instantly and looked forward to it daily. As he entered the studio, it was the second thing to strike his senses, just after the vibrant light spilling from within.

"Do you guys ever sleep?" It seemed to Rick that both El and Alma were always at Zivot, and maybe they were, but what was even more impressive to Rick was the level of energy they maintained. Neither seemed to ever lack in energy, wisdom, or the unexpected.

"Rick, my boy, Zivot is too exciting to sleep for very long." El lifted a glass of orange juice from one of the paint-covered tables, raising it as if to toast to the greatness of the studio. As he lowered the glass, a short but deep cough escaped him, and El instinctively braced his chest.

There was an undeniable frailty in his posture — a contradiction to his lively spirit. El's energy was there, but it seemed to be masked by an underlying condition. And that cough — it lingered in Rick's mind as an unsettling reminder that something wasn't right.

A small hot plate and waffle iron were on the table, plugged into an extension cord that looked too old to be safe. Elements of the wires peeked through the worn black plastic sheath of the cord, which had been held together for years with little more than hope and black electrical tape.

"Do you guys do this every morning? Breakfast in the studio, I mean."

"Not every day, but it's one of my favorite things," said Alma. "I swear, there are some places where breakfast just tastes better."

"I agree," Rick said, recalling breakfasts from his boyhood camping trips in the mountains of Idaho. There was something about cooking on an open flame, the crisp mountain air, and the invigorating scent of pine trees on the breeze — a taste that simply couldn't be replicated.

El interrupted his thoughts and handed Rick a thin paper plate with a fresh waffle and glass of orange juice. A cut of butter melted between the square lines of the waffle, then lifted above the syrup as Rick prepared to eat. It wasn't the same as camp food, but it was nonetheless amazing.

After a bit of small talk, El turned more serious. "Rick, why are you here?"

Rick sat stunned. "What do you mean? You brought me here, remember? The night in the rain, the blank canvas?"

"No, that's not what I mean," El said with a bite of a waffle.

Rick paused. He felt his brow furrow with contemplation. Up until that moment, he figured it was just something to do since losing his job, but the question caused him to really think.

"I guess you're teaching me to look at the world differently. Everything up to this point in my life felt like it was so surface level. You've taught me to think differently and pay attention to things that I never did before," Rick shrugged, wondering if that was the right answer.

"So, you're not just chasing Alma?" El bantered.

"I think she might be chasing me," Rick said, feeling his face flush. Alma gave him a flirty wink. He was a bit surprised that she played along.

El backed up, playfully sickened by the flirting. "I think you're misunderstanding me. Why are you here on this little rock, spinning around in space?"

Alma's eyebrows raised in question.

El raised a hand to his chest, quieting another cough that rattled deep in his lungs. Rick made eye contact with Alma, sensing her concern.

El gathered himself. His point wasn't getting through. "Think beyond now Rick, beyond this moment. Why are you here on earth? Why are you alive right now? If you can't answer that, you may not be ready for the next step."

Rick hesitated again. He should have known El was talking about something more than just art. He was referring again to the art of life.

"I don't know, El. How can anyone know?"

Rick could tell that El appreciated his honesty. "You're right, Rick. How can anyone truly know? But what if you decided, right now, what your purpose was — even if it wasn't exactly right? Wouldn't it be better to have something to guide you, even temporarily, than to drift aimlessly waiting for an answer?"

Rick felt a wave of embarrassment. He knew it was an important question, but he had no clear answer. Sure, he'd thought about it before, but only fleetingly. "I guess... I want to make a difference. I'd like to make a difference in the lives of others."

El nodded, a small smile forming. "That's a good start, Rick. If you look at nearly any survey about what makes a meaningful life, five things consistently show up: family, friends, career, health, and purpose. But purpose," El emphasized, "is the thread that ties the others together. It gives meaning to everything we do."

Rick listened intently as El continued, "Until you find your purpose, may I make a suggestion?"

Rick's eyebrows lifted with curiosity. "Sure," he replied.

"I believe we're here to create — to create amazing moments within our relationships, paths to new adventures, visions that inspire, and journeys that transform us. Would you embrace that? Creation isn't easy; it challenges us to take everything life throws our way and shape it into something meaningful. But when you reframe challenges as just another stroke in your masterpiece, the sting fades, and the picture becomes even more powerful."

Rick paused, considering El's words. "Create, huh?" he said thoughtfully, his tone softening. "I've never really thought about it that way, but it makes sense. I'd give it a try," Rick agreed without hesitation. El's suggestions, though sometimes eccentric, had always proven practical.

El smiled. "Life is filled with opportunities for artistry, but ultimately, we're the ones responsible for developing our own world — especially during times of change. You're here with us now because your last canvas ran out of space. Think about how exciting that is."

As he spoke, El began tidying up their breakfast. He put away extra paper plates and utensils, wiped batter spills from the table, and cleaned drips from the sides of the waffle iron. His movements were thoughtful, as if the act of cleaning helped him gather his thoughts.

"What most people never seem to grasp," El continued, his voice steady, "is that they get to choose the course of their own storyline. They decide the direction. They determine how long to carry a point forward based on the attention they give it. Some people drag things out far too long; others abandon them before they've barely begun."

He paused, glancing at Rick and Alma, as though weighing their reactions. "But the truth is, most people give up too soon when inspiration strikes. Creating can be draining. It demands every ounce of energy you have."

El adjusted a jar of brushes, his hand lingering thoughtfully. "Actually, most people don't know what they want to create."

"So how do you find that, El? Where do you start?" Alma asked with sincerity. "You feel something stirring beneath the surface, but you're not sure where to go with it." The question drew Rick's attention. He glanced at her, unsure if she was speaking for herself or subtly steering him toward a lesson she already knew.

El paused, shifting his focus to Alma. Then he leaned forward, his voice steady. "The next part of your journey doesn't have to be perfectly laid out, but you do need a sense of direction. Creation is a process of discovery. It rewards action."

He paused. "Think of it like a blank canvas. The first stroke doesn't define the whole image, but it sets everything in motion. The artist begins to see the next stroke as they complete the prior — it's a process that unfolds. You don't need to have it all figured out — just take that first step and let the journey begin."

"So where do you start?" Alma pressed, her tone more firm than usual, catching Rick off guard. It was the first time he'd sensed anything other than her usual pleasantness. Known as a wanderer, her question seemed fitting.

El leaned back, his tone steady, and met Alma's gaze. "I can give you a start," he said, "but I can't take the artistry of discovery from you. That's something you have to create for yourself." He let the words linger, then continued, his expression thoughtful.

"Figuring out what you want starts with a few simple questions. What's missing in your life? What lights you up, or makes you feel alive? Think back to the moments that mattered most — what were you doing, and why did it feel important? Look for the threads that connect those moments."

He gestured lightly, as if sketching a canvas in the air. "From there, picture what a fulfilling life might look like — not perfect, just something that feels right. Write it down, let it shift and grow over time. The answers will come, but only if you're willing to start exploring."

Rick watched as the look in El's eyes changed from a distant daydream to focusing on the lighting above him.

El gathered himself, "See that light bulb?"

Rick and Alma followed El's gaze upward. The ceiling was lined with long fluorescent tubes, their white glow casting an even light across the room. El pointed to one of the fixtures. "It's not a masterpiece, but it gets the job done, doesn't it?" He leaned back, tapping one finger on his chin in a thoughtful pause before turning his attention back to Rick.

"Yeah, I guess so?" Rick's statement came out as a question, unsure what El's point was.

"Do you realize," El mused, his eyes fixed on the lights above, "that Edison tried thousands of times before he felt the light bulb was ready for the world? He didn't have an exact path forward — he was charting new territory. But he had an idea he believed was worth exploring. We all have ideas, but most people give up long before a thousand attempts.

"Most people understand the lesson of persistence in Edison's work, but there's another, equally important lesson that almost no one considers."

Rick glanced at Alma and could tell she was searching for the hidden lesson but coming up empty.

"Most of us think we have to wait for the perfect conditions before we begin something. Not Edison! He knew that sometimes you just have to start. The perfect moment, the perfect result — those rarely come."

Alma nodded.

"Even when Edison finally had a design that could create light, it still had its shortcomings. But he moved forward with production anyway — and in doing so, he lit up the world. It wasn't perfect. It could have been improved. Think about how many versions of the light bulb we've seen since 1879. What if he had waited for the ideal creation?"

He let the question hang in the air before continuing.

"Edison had the courage to begin with what he had. He didn't invent LED lights, smart lighting, or fluorescent tubes. But with a single line of carbonized bamboo filament, he revolutionized the world."

"Can you imagine if he'd waited for everything to be just right?"

"He never would have found it," Alma said, breaking the silence.

"Exactly. If Edison had waited for everything to fall into place, we'd still be sitting in darkness, yearning for something better than candlelight. Sometimes chasing an ideal solution does more harm than moving forward with what's good enough to start."

Alma added, "It's like that first confident line on a canvas — you don't always know what it'll become, but you trust it enough to keep going."

El smiled. "Exactly. That first bulb wasn't polished or flashy by today's standards, but by any standard, Edison's actions were courageous. With a single line of filament, he didn't just create light — he gave the world a direction.

"And from there? Momentum took over. And momentum — more than anything — is what fuels progress, innovation, and lasting change."

Rick was struck that something as revolutionary as the light bulb was merely a starting point rather than a flawless product. He had one last question. "Okay, so once you build momentum, gain speed, and your plan takes flight, how do you maintain that?"

It was a profound question, one that deserved explanation.

El's excitement grew somber. "Excellent question, Rick. I have a friend who learned that lesson the hard way. Let me tell you about him."

CHAPTER 9

ONE DEGREE

El hurried over to an old military-surplus cabinet tucked away in the dimly lit corner of the warehouse, beyond the reach of the fluorescent lights. He gently tugged on the metal-beaded cord of the lamp that sat on top. It wasn't a lot, but it gave enough light to see. The cabinet, weathered by time and purpose, stood as the divine protector of El's artistic treasures. Within the sturdy cabinet, he had haphazardly stowed an array of art supplies, brushes, and an assortment of odds and ends, each with its own story waiting until a spark of inspiration would call on them.

With a sense of purpose, El's hands danced over the cabinet's drawers. Each drawer held a limitless potential of creativity. As he rifled through the compartments, the clinks and rustles of the tools echoed through the warehouse, a symphony of artistic inspiration. After a brief exploration, he emerged triumphant, clutching a metal ruler. Its cool surface was pitted and splattered with various art products, a testament to the countless projects it had aided.

El continued, "You asked how to maintain the momentum. Momentum isn't just about moving fast — it's about never stopping the process of learning, refining, and pushing forward. It's about continually moving forward."

Rick listened, thinking about times in his own life when he had started something but lost steam — ideas abandoned before they could evolve, projects that faded as excitement waned. He lost his curiosity for the project. He wanted quick wins to demonstrate he was going to be an overnight success. He always thought momentum meant speed — charging ahead at full force. But maybe it was less about the initial push and more about endurance — the ability to adapt when inspiration met resistance.

El continued, "It's about recognizing that every breakthrough is just a foundation for what comes next. And quite honestly, it's about course corrections. The moment you stop adjusting, questioning, or improving, momentum stalls, and what was once innovation becomes outdated.

"Think of it like a runner. Speed off the line matters, but if they don't adjust their stride, pace their energy, and push through fatigue, they burn out before the finish line. Innovation works the same way. The key isn't just starting — it's sustaining and maintaining course."

Rick nodded, a new realization settling in. "So momentum isn't just movement — it's movement with intention."

"Exactly," El said. "And those who master that? They don't just make discoveries, they change the world."

El paused, reflective. "What do you two know about navigation?"

Rick and Alma exchanged a glance.

"Without GPS, I'd be in trouble," Alma admitted.

Rick nodded. "Same here."

El smiled knowingly. "There are two very important lessons I've learned. As the journey unfolds and you start to sense where you're headed, you need landmarks to keep your bearings. You can't just say, 'I'll keep my eyes on the horizon and follow it to success.'"

He leaned forward, his gaze locking onto Rick. "Why? Why can't you do that?"

Rick hesitated, then answered slowly. "Because the horizon doesn't exist. It's not a fixed point — it's just a..." His words trailed off, hovering between a question and a realization.

El nodded. "Go deeper — why doesn't it exist?"

Rick took a breath, more comfortable as the student than the teacher. "A horizon line isn't real. It's an illusion. A horizon line's an illusion. The more you move toward it, the more it moves away."

"Exactly," El said. "Horizon lines, like success, are illusions. What feels like success today might look completely different tomorrow. Even people who seem highly successful often feel like they've come up short, because both success and perspective shift over time. Others get distracted from what they originally set out to do. That's why, once you know where you're headed, you need fixed points. They help you measure progress and make sure you're still on course."

El nodded slowly, almost to himself. "Anyone can draw a straight line in short bursts. But the longer you draw it out, the more likely you are to drift away from your starting point or even lose sight of why you began in the first place. That's when things get off track. You have to be ready to make adjustments as time goes on."

Rick thought back to his corporate days. Organizations always had big, long-term goals, but they measured their progress in short, measurable objectives. As long as their immediate goals were aligned with their end goal, they provided reasonable mile markers along the way. He had never done that in his own life — instead, he fixated on long-range plans, often feeling he had come up short when, in truth, more often than not, he was hitting key milestones along the way. It was when he got distracted that he strayed off course.

El paused, his eyes glistening with emotion as memories stirred. "Course corrections," he said, his voice steady, "will always be part of the process."

 "A good friend of mine was a pilot during the war. Just a kid, really, but he carried the massive responsibility of delivering supplies to the front lines. Every leader knows how critical the front lines are — it's where everything happens, and so many were dependent on him. He had big plans and goals for after the war, things he wanted to accomplish. But he never made it home.

As you can imagine his parents were devastated. They wanted answers. They pressed the military for years, and the best explanation they got was that his plane was off course. His entire existence came down to the '1 in 60 rule.'"

"The 1 in 60 rule?" Rick was confused.

"It's an aviation term that pilots are taught. It basically says that if a path is charted just 1 degree off course and you follow that path for 60 miles, you will be 1 mile off your target by the time you land. He was flying for hours, so whether he was 1 degree off or 10 degrees off target, we'll never know. The point is, no one knows where he landed and he was never found."

El shook his head almost in disbelief. "My friend was likely so far off course that he just ran out of fuel. That's like a lot of us. By the time we realize we are off target, many — like my friend — run out of gas, or are so far off track that they give up hope or don't reach their destination. You've got to keep your goal in sight."

His gaze then fell upon a large piece of artboard, waiting patiently for the touch of El's skilled hand. With purposeful intent, he pulled the board toward him at the table to begin his work. In that moment, Rick swore that he visually saw a spark of creative energy jump from El's pen to the artboard, signaling that the artist was about to impart another piece of wisdom.

"Come here," he said, waving his hands frantically, like he was directing his pilot friend where to land. "Let's say you start here," El continued, pointing to the lower left corner of the artboard. He wrote "Origin," and sketched a military base with far too much precision for such a simple lesson. Then he walked around to the opposite side of the oversized board and wrote "Destination," drawing an airstrip beneath it.

But El didn't stop there. Ever the artist, he worked feverishly, creating a detailed model of the military base and the future destination. It was a bit much, but Rick couldn't help but marvel at the artwork and how quickly El effortlessly brought the scene to life.

El then handed Rick the ruler he had retrieved earlier from the cabinet. "Now, use this to draw a line connecting the two points," he said. The artboard was large, forcing Rick to reposition it and adjust the ruler over and over to complete the line.

"There, a perfectly straight line," Rick said with playful sarcasm, knowing full well that perfection didn't exist. He grinned as he teased El, leaning into his prior lessons.

Using Rick's charted line as a guide, El used a protractor to chart other paths 1 degree, 3 degrees, and 5 degrees off course and then extended those lines to show how far off course his friend could have strayed.

"Always remember, while there is power in a line, that power can be devastating if you're not intentional about what you're aligned to."

Rick frowned, the words hitting a little too close to home. "Are you saying one deviation can ruin everything? The layoff was a deviation I hadn't anticipated. Are you saying I can't recover?"

El's expression softened, and he shook his head. "No, not at all, Rick. Let me show you something."

He handed Rick the pen again. "Remember, I told you anyone can draw a straight line in short bursts. But now, I want you to freehand a straight line from the origin to the destination."

Rick nodded and placed the pen at the origin, carefully moving it toward the destination point. As the line extended, he had to stretch, and without the ruler as a guide, the line began to wobble. He paused, regrouped, and redirected toward the point.

When they stepped back, it was clear to everyone that the line wasn't perfectly straight, but it connected the two points.

"See, Rick? A deviation doesn't ruin the whole picture, but it can change the course. That's why corrections matter — just like the ones you made. In life, sometimes we drift off track without realizing it. Other times, something forces us onto an entirely different path, like your layoff. Either way, it's up to us to adapt."

Rick's adjusted line began to glow with an electric-blue vibrance, a stamp of approval on the corrections that were made.

El gestured toward the canvas and its glow. "The key is owning the line you're drawing, even when it strays from your original plan. Remember what I said: It's easy to draw straight lines in short bursts, but any line extended far enough will eventually drift. That's why, when you have long-term goals, you have to be especially mindful and ready to adjust.

"When a line goes astray, we don't scrap the entire work — we adjust, incorporate it, or correct its course. We make it part of the design. Life works the same way. It's about staying true to your direction through thoughtful corrections, and sometimes it's about embracing the detour when it leads to something better. That could be where you're headed Rick, something better."

El looked intently between Rick and Alma. "Unfortunately, my friend didn't make the necessary adjustments. Whether he didn't notice he was off course, or thought he didn't need to correct, the result was the same — at some point, he lost momentum and ran out of gas."

"How do you know when to make corrections?" Rick asked, his tone curious yet serious.

"Great question." El's eyes lit up with thoughtfulness. "If you do anything long enough, you develop a feel for it — but only if you're paying attention. Some of it is trial and error, but with time, you'll learn. I have four questions I ask myself whenever I'm contemplating a change."

El turned to the "1 in 60" artboard. At the top, he drew a small hashtag, followed by the number 1. With a few quick strokes, he sketched an erratic, wandering line that looped aimlessly across the page.

"First," he began, "do I have direction? Is this trajectory taking me closer to or farther from my target? A line without direction is just a scribble — it goes nowhere. If the path feels right, but a small adjustment can realign me, it's better to correct now rather than when I am way off course."

He drew another hashtag with the number 2 and a flame. "Second, am I spending more energy than what I get in return, or am I burning out? If there's no spark it might be time to reconsider."

After drawing the next hashtag and number 3, he sketched a question mark, its curve precise. "Third, are my actions causing harm to me or others? If they are, it's time to change course. A good line, Rick, should build, not break."

He paused briefly, writing the last hashtag and a number 4. He then drew a square around a blank space on the page. "And finally, sometimes it's not the line that needs fixing. It may just be time for a new canvas. Ask yourself: Is this canvas complete? Have you given it all you can? Sometimes it's not about adjustments — it's about starting fresh."

El placed the pen down and looked at Rick. Rick was already contemplating where he would chart his next course.

CHAPTER 10

LEADING LINES AND GUIDELINES

It felt like ages since Rick had shared golden-brown waffles with El and Alma. Since then, his approach had deepened — he was taking his study of lines more seriously, and his skills were starting to reflect it. In recent days, El had begun pushing him further, introducing more advanced concepts like contours and shading to create the illusion of three-dimensional form.

Today Rick started with the simple outline of an apple. With smooth, contoured lines, he began to add roundness and depth to the flat shape. Each stroke varied in pressure, creating a balance between thick and thin lines that hinted at dimension. These curved accents followed the apple's natural contours, simulating the play of a light source to give it a three-dimensional form.

With meticulous movements, he added layers of lines to enhance the apple's depth. Where the intersecting lines overlapped, the darkness hinted at shadows. Open areas of paper served as highlights.

Without being taught, Rick explored the principle of crosshatching. He discovered where lines intersect and overlap to depict the darkest points. Gradually, as he added more lines, a gradient emerged, transitioning smoothly from light to dark, bringing the apple to life.

"Hmmm... looking good."

Rick jolted. He hadn't noticed his mentor approach, let alone lean over his shoulder to study the drawing.

"Geez, El. You nearly gave me a heart attack."

But El was too focused on the drawing to respond. Reaching around Rick, he pointed to an arrow of shadowing.

"Pay attention to that, Rick. As you go through the apprenticeship, notice areas of intersecting lines — places where paths cross, principles meet, or lessons repeat. There's strength there. These intersections create depth. When you see overlap, you're witnessing a pattern. It creates emphasis. Just like on paper, it's been my experience that the Great Creator of this cosmic canvas uses patterns to point something out to us. If we pay attention, life might use them to draw our attention to a purpose — or we might recognize patterns in our own behavior causing events to unfold."

Rick continued to draw as they spoke.

What had started as a flat sketch now popped off the page, a tangible, glossy fruit brought to life. Rick had left several areas untouched, plain paper contrasting the dark overlapping contour lines. This created an illusion of reflected light — the apple seemed to gleam.

"What do you mean by that? Patterns of our own behavior?" Rick paused his drawing.

"Some people like to blame others for their misfortunes. Take the guy who curses the cop for giving him a ticket — but that same guy constantly drives ninety miles per hour on the freeway. Whose fault was it really? The driver is the one who crossed the line. The cop just witnessed it. There are all kinds of examples like that. If you find yourself dealing with the same situations over and over again, it could be a sign that you need to make a change."

Then El smiled, dangling a set of keys. "Speaking of speeding, want to go for a ride?"

Curious, Rick followed him outside. The sunlight hit the polished curves of a pristine, yellow 1974 Corvette Stingray. The car was a work of art that demanded respect — aggressive yet elegant. Unlike today's cars, the headlights were concealed in the hood, giving the machine a sleek and commanding profile.

El climbed in the driver's seat.

Rick had never seen El look so completely out of place, yet entirely in his element. The older white man in a pristine muscle car — it was a stereotype Rick would never have imagined for him. But then again, why would El drive anything less than a masterpiece?

After a moment's hesitation, Rick nodded and slid into the passenger seat. The scent of leather and motor oil replaced the ink and canvas of the studio.

The door shut with a satisfying thump, and El fired up the engine. It growled to life — confident, alive. Rick had barely buckled before the tires squealed, launching them forward.

For the first stretch, neither spoke. The city blurred by, but just as quickly as it shot off, the car came to a screeching halt in front of a nearby street light.

"That's the problem with having a car like this in New York," El mused. "You never really get a chance to let her run the way she was meant to. It's like taking an eagle and putting it in a cage its whole life, with no open space to fly."

"What a beauty," Rick said, running a hand along the dashboard.

El nodded, eyes still fixed ahead. "It was a gift from someone who realized he couldn't take it with him. He was sick — didn't have long. And when people reach that place, they stop gripping so tightly. Cars, collections, grudges — none of it matters as much."

"You knew him well?" Rick asked, confused by the statement.

"Not well," El said, "but well enough. He wanted it in the exhibit."

"The exhibit?" Rick repeated, with a furrowed brow.

El turned the vehicle into a shadowed alley, and Rick's nerves prickled. Rick frowned. The alley felt wrong — narrow, off-balance — like they'd crossed into a space where lines might be crossed and rules bent. His heart beat a little faster in anticipation. The space felt different — tighter, shadowed, flanked by looming warehouses that seemed to press inward. If it had been night, his instincts would have been to run.

As they approached an unfamiliar building, El rolled down the window. Chains clanked and metal screeched as a large industrial garage door rolled open.

Someone approached the vehicle. A man Rick vaguely recognized greeted them. His eyes locked on the mechanic's shirt — navy blue, with a stitched name tag that read "Nando." Rick blinked. The rain. The alley. It was the man who had warned Rick the first night in the rain, when he bought the canvas. It was him. He had the same ponytail, the same steady presence — only now, the scowl had been replaced by something else entirely — a grin.

"You made it," the man said.

El laughed, shifting the car into park. "Of course I did, Fernando. Was there any doubt?"

Fernando smirked, shifting his stance like a pit-crew chief ready to call the shots. "Doubt? Nah, not with you, my friend. You always deliver. Pull up under the lights — you've got the last pole position tonight. We've cleared a path just for you."

Nando's hands moved with practiced precision, guiding El into the building like a racer entering the pits. Every sharp, deliberate motion reflected the focus of someone who lived and breathed speed and control.

El released the clutch and gradually let the car roll forward. Rick tensed. What was this place? A chop shop? Had El stolen the car?

"Welcome to Hashwork," El said, reading his mind. "An underground art movement. We call this exhibit 'Changing Lanes.'"

The expansive building was alive inside — transformed into an underground art gallery. Spotlights, exhibits, catering tables, and dozens of people all moving with purpose, tightening up finishing touches.

El coughed hoarsely, a sharp edge to it, then cleared his throat as if to shake it off and quickly moved on.

"There's a very eclectic audience that attends. Each event has almost a rock-and-roll vibe. Everyone wants to be a part of something bigger than themselves; they want to break free, so people come from all over. You see, Rick, we attract a lot of people like you — businesspeople who want something different. What makes this special is the atmosphere; the art adds to it, but it's also the building, its history, and the people who gather in it."

They exited the vehicle; the air smelled like old oil and fresh paint. Someone bumped a stereo knob, and the hum of a distant highway rose up — sounds of cars flying past, tires on the pavement, as if the room itself was remembering its prior life as an auto shop.

Nearby was a display of old, shredded maps, stitched back together with red thread. Each stitch marked a detour — but held the maps together. A plaque read, "The roads I chose — and the ones I didn't — all led here."

Rick smiled. Of all the places he'd imagined ending up, this wasn't one of them.

His eyes dropped to the floor — bold double yellow lines cut through the concrete, mimicking a highway.

They swept through the space in wide arcs, then tightened into sharp turns — guiding visitors past art installations and showcase pieces with deliberate precision.

El caught Rick's inquisitive look and smirked. "I told you, Rick, lines are a powerful thing. Watch tonight — no one will tell them to, but every person who walks through those doors will follow those lines. Conditioned to stay in their lane, they'll stick to the path, even when it doesn't make sense." He paused. "Well, most will."

"Isn't that what you want? To guide people through the exhibit?"

"Absolutely. We're using those lines to guide traffic. A principle called leading lines. In the art world, we use it to guide the viewer to a focal point of attention."

Rick turned. Fernando stood there, arms crossed, his presence steady as bedrock. "Lines can lead us, sure — but if you don't know who painted them, how can you trust where they go? Especially when you throw a little high-octane into the mix. Right, El?"

Rick felt the weight of the statement. It wasn't just about the lines — it was about intent, trust, and whether the paths we follow are really our own.

El nodded. "More dangerous is aligning with a vision that isn't yours. Most people follow a path someone else created, and they're miserable for it. Thank goodness for a blank canvas."

The highway-like lines of the exhibit pulsed electric blue, baiting Rick forward.

El and Fernando nodded to one another knowingly, as if they shared a secret from a past life.

Rick continued forward, eyes tracing the painted lines beneath his feet.

How many times had he driven down roads without knowing who laid the lines or where they truly led?

He thought about the paths he'd followed in life. Some drawn by friends. Others by family. And more than a few by strangers with loud opinions and clever captions on social media.

As he suspected, the lines wound back and forth within the confines of the expansive warehouse. In the background and through hidden speakers, the exhibitors played the audio of engines revving, tires squealing, and other automotive sounds. At various points, he could smell the scent of motor oil.

Everything added to the ambience, but his favorite moment was when he approached an exhibit designed to embrace the nostalgia of Little Trees — those iconic cardboard air fresheners, usually seen dangling from rearview mirrors.

The artist had taken a clever twist and transformed the familiar Little Trees into towering giants, each standing at least eight feet tall. Despite their enormous size, they retained the same texture and scent that were so deeply etched in Rick's memory. He leaned in close to the yellow tree. For a moment, the unmistakable scent of vanilla overpowered the oil in the air, leaving a broad grin on his face.

Continuing on, the path guided him past various partitions and exhibits filled with sculptures, paintings, carvings, drawings, canvases, easels, and countless auto parts, many of which he didn't recognize. Rick was astonished by the sheer length of the path and the scale of the exhibit.

Then, without warning, his journey took an unexpected turn.

He came upon a display titled "The Crossroads."

At first, it seemed straightforward: a yellow, diamond-shaped road sign marked with intersecting black lines. A standard crossroads — the kind he'd passed a hundred times on backroads in Idaho without giving it a second thought.

But this time, it wasn't alone.

Four identical signs appeared, each subtly altered, each framed with intention.

The second sign, unlike the first, sat between the letters S and U. The intersecting lines now resembled the letter T. When paired with the numbers 4 and 5, the symbol transformed — no longer a crossroads, but a calculation. A choice waiting to be made.

He turned to the third sign — this one rotated 45 degrees. Flanked by the letters W and Y, the symbol became an X. And between two numbers, it suggested multiplication. Potential. Growth. Something small becoming more.

Then it struck him.

None of the signs had changed — only their surroundings had. A slight rotation, a shift in framing. The signs were identical. But when viewed differently, they told entirely new stories.

It wasn't the symbol that carried the meaning — it was the context around it.

A crossroads wasn't a dead end. It wasn't even just a choice.

It was an invitation: to calculate, to multiply, to redefine what comes next.

He remembered what he'd learned earlier: interpretation gives meaning. But now, something deeper clicked. Maybe that's why they say hindsight is 20/20 — because only when you look back do you see the events that framed the moment in front of you.

It wasn't just about interpreting what something meant.

It was about realizing that even your first interpretation could be challenged, reshaped — reframed.

It wasn't a revelation — it was a reframing. And that changed everything.

Rick continued through the exhibit, taking in the brilliant colors and clean lines of spectacular vehicles, following the path that had been laid out, until eventually the path narrowed into a small, dark room — a dead end.

Rick remembered Fernando's warning: Be careful whose line you follow. The dead end felt abrupt — sudden and out of place. It was the last thing he'd expected. The room he now found himself in was dark, too dark to see. He considered turning back to where he'd come from, but reasoned there must be purpose, even in this dead end.

With hands outstretched, he pressed against the pitch-black walls, searching for a way forward. Just when it seemed the space had closed in completely — that he might be stuck — his fingers found an opening. A hidden door.

A slow smile crept across his face as he stepped out of the darkness — where El, Alma, and a host of others from the studio were waiting. They applauded.

It was the ultimate lesson — when you hit a dead end, creativity finds a way.

He wondered how the other attendees would respond. Would they follow the lines without question, lulled forward by the design, or freeze at the abrupt stop? Would they turn back? Search for another way? Or simply stand there, lost?

Laughter broke the silence of his thoughts. El's was light and full of life, while Fernando's carried the deep timbre of an idling engine.

"You're a good sport, Rick," El said, grinning. "Everything's working exactly as planned. Tonight's going to be fun."

The point was clear now. The world is filled with leading lines — subtle paths that shape choices, steer beliefs, and quietly dictate direction. But the real power wasn't in following them. It was in recognizing when to step off the road and create your own.

But the laughter faded as El stumbled, catching himself with a sharp cough. His lips turned slightly blue.

Fernando was there in an instant, steadying him. No stool to break his fall this time.

"Come on, let's sit for a minute," Fernando said, gripping El's arm.

Rick watched as El's gaze drifted — distant, as if there were something he wasn't saying.

El's hands rested on the table, his fingers tracing the linear grain of the wood as if searching for the right words. Rick could tell he wanted to speak.

"Are you okay, El? You don't look so good."

"I'll be fine," El said, trying to reassure him. But Rick could tell by the look on Alma and Fernando's faces — they weren't so sure.

Even after El caught his breath, he stayed seated at the table, drained — no matter how hard he tried to hide it. As guests began arriving, he remained quiet, offering the occasional smile, but his weariness was hard to miss.

Finally, as the exhibit filled, El stood.

He steadied himself. His hand rested on Rick's shoulder a moment too long before giving a gentle push.

"Enjoy tonight," he said softly, his voice rough. "You've earned it."

Rick hesitated, but Alma tugged him gently by the hand, urging him to explore — mingle, watch, observe.

Just as El had predicted, the guests moved through the exhibit with eerie synchronicity. They followed the path without hesitation, unaware — or perhaps uninterested — in who had designed it. Something unseen drew them forward, their curiosity tethered to the lines on the floor like threads on a spool.

Rick watched, unsure if their obedience came from trust, faith, or habit.

In the end, it didn't matter.

The people followed.

CHAPTER 11

A CRITIQUE FOR THE CRITICS

Rick's morning hadn't started as he'd hoped. After an early game of pickleball at a nearby park, he dropped onto a bench to catch his breath and rehydrate. He had never anticipated the level of intensity the game could demand — or that he'd find himself this winded. Like so many others in America, Rick had recently fallen in love with pickleball.

What he loved most was its versatility. He could play casually and still have fun, or he could go all in when competition demanded. This morning's match required the latter.

After the final game, Rick skimmed the morning news on his phone. Most headlines blurred together — until a local story brought him to an abrupt stop.

His blood boiled as he read. The article hit hard, the title cutting like it had been written just for him. It was as if some social media algorithm or the universe itself had conspired to deliver this moment.

It read, "Local High-Octane Art Stalls at the Starting Line." Rick knew instantly it was about El and the studio. A wave of frustration surged through him, but he kept reading, his determination mounting with every word.

"What had all the promise of a high-end luxury ride felt more like a Ford Pinto." Rick wasn't a car guy, but he knew the reference. The Ford Pinto of the 1970s was a catastrophic failure of car design. He had long heard stories about fiery explosions when the car was rear-ended, caused by the placement of the gas tank.

"You don't have to be a gearhead to appreciate the beauty and clean lines of a well-designed vehicle. Last night's underground art exhibit, hosted by Zivot Studio and the friends of local artist, "El," had hoped to take visitors on a thrilling exploration of the revving masterpiece of an intersection between speed, design, and art, but instead delivered an experience that felt more like a stalled engine and bad exhaust.

"The central pieces — a series of deconstructed cars and automotive parts had been arranged in dramatic poses. Along a supposedly winding roadway, the journey was meant to take travelers across a sweeping exhibit, hoping to evoke a sense of motion and innovation. Yet, the emotional torque left most feeling idle. Instead, the sweeping roadway designed to guide visitors, more often than not, came to a bottleneck as travelers stopped far too often. While there were spectacular pieces on display, they were often lost in the congested bottlenecks and gridlocks.

"Instead of an exhilarating ride, it made this participant feel like she was stuck with a bad cabbie on the Brooklyn-Queens Expressway.

"The problem was not in the ambition of the concept, having attracted big-name designers such as Fernando Martinez, but the failure was in its execution. The installation leaned heavily on the aesthetic appeal of polished metal and sleek curves, yet delivered a ride that was slow and clunky. The cars were artfully reimagined, but the experience felt static and lifeless.

"Moreover, the attempt to use the cars as metaphors for human experience — speed as a stand-in for modern life's pace, or the vehicle as a symbol of freedom — came across as forced and superficial. The lack of subtlety in this metaphor rendered the installation as more of a literal interpretation than an invitation for deeper thought.

"The highlight of the event was one that many may not have appreciated. The creativity of Zivot Studio had pumped in a dynamic soundscape of revving engines and screeching tires, intended to heighten the immersive experience. A subtle hint of motor oil was carefully hidden away and diffused into the air to give the room depth without overwhelming the senses. If anything, these elements were too understated.

"The biggest disappointment, however, was the poorly thought-out design of the road, which brought an already slow ride to a screeching halt as the roadway ended at an abrupt and dead-end wall.

"In the end, this 'High-Octane Art Installation' turned out to be a lemon — a flashy, ambitious concept that sputtered out with bad gas."

Without a word to his playing partners, Rick shoved his paddle into his backpack, slung it over his shoulder, and sprinted toward Zivot Studio.

Already worn out from the game, Rick felt heavy droplets of sweat gather on his forehead and cascade down his face. They ran across his furrowed brow, around his eyes, and down the bridge of his nose.

Though he ran with purpose, his apprenticeship had trained him to notice the smallest details in life. He observed how his eyebrows diverted sweat from his eyes. He felt drops cross the bridge of his nose, then follow the crease between his nostrils and cheeks. Two drops raced along the curve of his lips before merging at his chin and falling in unison.

The chaotic yet controlled pattern of the droplets triggered a memory from his youth. He thought of watching The Price Is Right, where contestants played games for prizes. His favorite was Plinko, where contestants released wooden pucks down a giant pegboard. The pucks ricocheted unpredictably, their paths diverted by pegs, until they landed in various quadrants.

But unlike Plinko, Rick wasn't chasing a prize. He was running with purpose, the weight of the article pushing him forward. He had to show El, so he quickened his pace.

The article was still fresh in Rick's mind as he arrived at the studio. He was too consumed by his emotion to pay attention to the warm glow he normally longed for. In a fit of anger, he swung the door open and marched in, ready to defend his friend and mentor.

"Have you seen this!" Rick exclaimed. "Can you believe what they are saying?"

Rick's frantic exclamations weren't received; in fact, they weren't even heard. A small group of artists and volunteers from the underground exhibit were gathered together, huddled around a tablet at a nearby table with Fernando and El. El was reading the review out loud.

Rick was surprised by the reaction of the group. They didn't even appear to be upset. As they read, they sat quietly, occasionally even laughing.

As El read the final line aloud, "In the end, this High-Octane Art Installation turned out to be a lemon — a flashy, ambitious concept that sputtered out with bad gas," a round of laughter rippled through the group.

Fernando raised his hand, patting El on the back. "Oh, brother, that's a good one — probably her best closing yet," he said with a grin. The group snickered together.

Rick's face tightened in confusion. "Wait — you mean you aren't upset? That doesn't bother you, having someone talk all that trash? The event was incredible!"

Fernando and El exchanged a knowing look, their smiles only brightening.

"Of course we care," El said, "but we care less because we know where it came from."

Rick tilted his head. "What do you mean? You know the author?"

"Sure," El replied, completely unfazed. "Spend enough time as an artist, and your path will eventually cross hers."

Rick hesitated, still piecing it together. Sensing his confusion — and the sting of his investment in the studio — El stepped forward, his tone gentle.

"Maybe this will help. I want you to meet someone who worked the event with us last night. Your paths probably didn't cross; there was a lot happening."

As he spoke, a woman in her late fifties stepped forward from the group gathered around the table. Silver hair, effortless confidence, that same sharp British accent...

Rick's stomach turned. He knew exactly who she was.

She had rescued him in class.

She had been the one to cut through the laughter, to call out the hecklers, to remind them what it felt like to be put on the spot.

And yet, standing here now, he realized — he didn't actually know who she was.

Before Rick could speak, El gestured toward her. "Rick, meet Emily Rockford."

She extended her hand with a warm smile. "A pleasure to meet you properly this time."

Rick hesitated before shaking it, his mind still catching up. "Wait, you mean *the* Emily Rockford?"

El's grin widened. "The one and only."

Rick exhaled, glancing at El. "You could've mentioned that earlier."

"And spoil the moment?" El chuckled. "Funny enough, Emily used to hold the same position as the author of that article you just read. In fact, she was her predecessor."

Rick blinked, stunned. The woman who had called out cynicism in the classroom had once been the source of it herself.

Emily smirked, reading his expression. "That's right. If you thought that article was harsh, you should've seen my work. I was downright brutal to people."

El raised his fist in mock frustration. "Why I oughta…"

Emily chuckled, crossing her arms. "El and I are friends now, but that wasn't always the case. I was brutal — not just to him, but to a lot of great artists."

Rick frowned, still wrapping his head around it. "But why? If you loved the arts, why tear people down?"

Emily sighed, leaning forward slightly. "Have you ever thought about the difference between a critic and a critique?"

Rick shook his head. "Not really."

"That's the problem." She exhaled. "We use words like critic, critique, and critical almost interchangeably, but they're not the same. Like El said, I used to be a critic — a professional one. But here's what I learned: criticism is often less about the art and more about getting attention."

Rick tilted his head, listening intently as Emily continued.

"When I started reporting, I loved the arts. I wanted to celebrate great work. But here's the truth: No one cared about glowing reviews. They went unnoticed. Positive words didn't sell papers."

El interjected, nodding. "Negativity gets attention. Always has."

"Exactly," Emily agreed. "My editor pulled me aside early in my career and told me that two things sell: sex and conflict. He told me to change my approach. So I did. The moment I started writing scathing reviews, I became relevant. People read my words, talked about them, shared them. I wasn't reviewing art anymore — I was stirring up controversy. Critics have learned to be critical because that's what gets attention in our society. But it also divides."

Rick studied her, suddenly understanding why she had stepped in that day. She had been where those students were. She had been where he was.

Emily turned to El and gestured toward his tablet. El, seeming to know where she was going, handed it to her without hesitation. She scrolled through the apps until she found one for digital drawing. Picking up the stylus, she selected a tool resembling a fine-point pen and drew a straight, clean horizon line across the screen.

Switching to a chisel-tipped marker, Emily dragged a jagged line downward from the horizon, carving a deep rupture into the earth. The shape was sharp, chaotic — splintering away from the balance above. It widened as it stretched, gaping and raw, before tapering into a fine crack that reached toward the viewer.

She turned the tablet toward Rick. Now the image was clear. Not just a crack. A fault line. A deep fracture splitting from the horizon, widening as it surfaced — threatening to tear everything apart.

"This is the one line you have to avoid at all costs," Emily said, her voice edged with frustration. "It's a fault line. Just like the critical review of the exhibition, it gets attention — but its purpose is to divide."

Rick studied the drawing, the widening split in the earth.

"You can literally watch it happen in real time," she continued. "Especially online. People gather on one side or the other, forming small armies — supporters, detractors. And as long as we engage, it only grows." She tapped the screen. "But imagine what could happen if we ever found a way to bridge the divide instead."

El watched, a proud smile tugging at the corner of his lips. His former student was now the teacher.

Rick leaned back, letting her words settle. "So no matter how great the event was, the author was always going to find something to criticize?"

As he spoke, the fault line pulsed, its ethereal blue glow flickering — splintering further, as if responding to the very idea of division.

Emily nodded. "Exactly. Faultfinding is easy. It's loud, brash, and it tears things down. But criticism and feedback aren't the same. True feedback builds. It challenges you to grow. It's the difference between destruction and refinement."

Rick frowned, turning the thought over. "So how do I know what to listen to?"

Emily softened. "That's the challenge, isn't it? The best way to avoid falling into a fault line — whether by finding fault with others or letting their opinions shake you — is to build a bridge. Start with empathy. Try to understand where they're coming from — even if you don't agree."

She continued, "Then comes the line of communication. Start by asking yourself, Is there any value here? Anything I can learn from? If yes, take it. If not, let it go. Not every opinion deserves your time, but some do. Just make sure you're responding, not reacting. Especially when you're trying something new, you need to protect your process. The loudest voices aren't always the wisest."

Rick nodded slowly, absorbing the weight of her words.

El stepped forward, reaching for the tablet. His eyes flicked over the fault line, considering. Then, with a few deliberate strokes, he made adjustments — sharpening the jagged edges, straightening the angles, tightening the breaks — until the fracture in the earth transformed into something else entirely.

Rick stood in awe. It was a lightning bolt now.

El held up the tablet, the transformed image alive with energy — no longer a fracture but a force of impact.

He turned to Rick, leaning in close, his voice steady, and emphatic.

"One thing you need to understand, Rick, is that the moment you begin to create — the moment you take up your pen, your brush, your canvas — you become a lightning rod. You will attract storms of negativity, but you will also hear the thunderous applause of those who see your work, and witness firsthand the sparks of change in those you inspire."

He paused.

"What you're looking at," El said, tapping the point where the bolt struck the ground, "is your impact line — the place where creation meets consequence. Where your work doesn't just exist — it moves people, shakes something loose in them, leaves a mark.

"No matter what you do in life — no matter what you create or the changes you make — you'll attract both critics and critiques as you attempt to rise above mediocrity. The key is learning to distinguish those who are trying to help from those who only intend to tear you down."

Fernando interjected, "And don't forget the worst critic, the one in your own head. Self-doubt is insidious. It doesn't just question you, it contradicts itself. Your mind is wired to protect you, but it's not always rational. One moment, it's telling you to play it safe. The next, it's asking why you haven't done more. Combine that inner conflict with listening to every outside voice, and you'll paralyze yourself before you even start."

Rick let the words settle. Fernando was right. The worst critic wasn't out there, it was the voice in his own head.

For the first time, Rick saw how fragile the line of communication truly is. It depends on two parties: the one speaking and the one listening. Without both, the line breaks. And even when both are present, the message can still morph, lost somewhere between intent and interpretation.

Communication wasn't clean. Not between individuals. And not within himself.

In fact, the most dangerous breakdown wasn't between people. It was the one happening inside his own mind.

The voice that questioned every move, that whispered doubt before a line was ever drawn.

He held both ends of the line of communication, speaker and listener, and still managed to twist the message. No interference. No outside noise. Just him and his thoughts. And at times, it was still a muddled mess.

El picked up where Fernando left off. "Even well-meaning feedback comes through someone else's lens. Their interpretation of your work isn't an absolute truth. It's just that — an interpretation. The real question is, which lines will you allow them to draw on your canvas?"

Fernando leaned back, closing the conversation. "Going back to your original question about the negative article — you asked if we cared. For me, that kind of criticism is easy to ignore. I know who wrote it, and I know why. Like Sun Tzu said, 'An evil enemy will burn his own nation to the ground to rule over the ashes.' If they want to cling to their ashes, let them. I'll keep my art. I get to choose my perspective."

CHAPTER 12

CONNECTING THE DOTS

Rick's phone buzzed against the edge of the worktable. He wiped his hands on a rag, smearing more ink than he cleaned off. The scent of oil paint and old brick clung to the air, mingling with the faint hum of artistic genius, those who had gone before him.

It had been months since he first walked into Zivot Studio, weeks since the car exhibit, and somehow, he was still here. His bank account wasn't growing, but at least he had stopped the bleeding — consulting where he could to cover expenses. He wasn't making what he used to, but for the first time in years, he had something else: time. And most of it, he spent here, surrounded by unfinished canvases, mismatched stools, and a handful of artists who felt more like family than the boardrooms he used to sit in.

He had always assumed he'd go back. But now, he wasn't so sure.

The screen on his smartphone lit up. Chase Mercer.

Rick let out an exasperated sigh. Their interactions had gone quiet since their awkward meeting at the deli, and he had assumed Chase was all talk. Just another guy flexing his success, throwing out vague promises. Rick never expected him to actually follow through.

He swiped to answer.

"Rickster!" Chase's voice boomed through the speaker. "Good news, man. I talked to my guys. They're ready to grow this thing — really blow it up. And they want you on board."

Rick hesitated. He never anticipated that Chase would ever get back to him. He was caught somewhere between excitement and dread — excitement for the paycheck, dread for what it would cost him. He could already see the zeros stacking back up in his account. If this thing worked, the money would be good. Really good. Nah, it would be great. But it would also mean leaving the studio behind — the mess, the ink stains, the version of himself he'd been trying to become.

Nearby, a chair scraped against the concrete floor. Life kept moving around him, but he stood still.

His fingers clenched, tightening around the phone as he glanced up. Across the room, Alma caught his eye. She smiled, brushing stray eraser shavings from a worktable and collecting various art tools. Just another ordinary moment — one of a thousand he'd shared here.

But if he took this job, moments like this would be erased from his daily schedule.

"Dude, are you still there? Hello?" Chase's voice cut through Rick's thoughts, sharp and sudden, like the paint knife El used to work thick layers of paint.

Rick exhaled, running a thumb over the ink smudges on his hand. "Yeah, I'm still here."

"So, what do you think, bro? You ready to get back in the game?"

Rick stared at his fingers, smudged with India ink, the kind that didn't wash off easily — a permanent reminder of the lessons he'd learned at Zivot, of the lines he'd drawn, not just on canvas, but in the choices that had redirected his life.

And yet, here he was.

Another line surfaced in the corner of his mind, as if clawing its way past the lessons he'd worked so hard to hold on to. It was a familiar line. A bold snaking curve, split by a vertical slash. A dollar sign.

It wasn't just a symbol. It was a decision. A habit. A pattern he thought he'd left behind.

And it pointed to the most logical, comfortable choice — the one that promised security but always left him feeling emotionally empty.

Rick hesitated, feeling the old tug — the gnawing fear that maybe he'd been playing artist when what he really needed was a paycheck.

Before he could stop himself, the words slipped out.

"Yeah, buddy. Let's do it!" Rick said, feeling it was the safer route —
another high-paying gig with potential.

"Yes! Let's go, my guy! Congratulations! This is gonna be big!" Chase's
voice cracked through the phone like a shot of caffeine — too loud, too
eager, too much. Rick had to pull the phone away from his ear.

"Wasn't sure if you'd go for it. Figured maybe you were still busy drawing
your pretty pictures." Chase laughed sharp and smug, then shifted, "Oh,
so what's the story with that girl from the deli?"

Rick heard him loud and clear. The deli question hit harder than Chase
could know.

He was referring to Alma. Rick knew he wouldn't be seeing her as often,
once he got back to work.

Rick didn't respond, but Chase kept talking anyway. "I'll have the team
draft a contract and work out a start date."

"Great, let's talk later, Chase." Rick ended the call without waiting for
a response.

The silence afterward felt louder than Chase's voice. Rick dropped onto
the stool, elbows on the table, head in his hands.

What had he just done?

The weight of it settled fast. Heavy. Familiar. Like slipping into an
old pair of boots — worn thin at the sole, but somehow still the
most comfortable.

Rick had never imagined channeling his energy into creativity or the
arts. He had once dismissed such pursuits as frivolous, reserved for
those less driven or serious about success. But now he realized how
wrong he had been. He had watched El, his mentor and friend, pour
himself tirelessly into his art with the same determination Rick had
once reserved for his career. Success, he began to understand, was not
a single, universal goalpost — it was as unique as the person pursuing it.

He looked up, catching movement across the room. Alma, straightening a stool, glanced at him with soft, curious eyes.

"You okay?" she asked.

Rick forced a smile, then lied. "Uh, yeah... just can't figure this one out." He gestured to the sketch in front of him, covering for the guilt and the commitment he had just made to Chase. On the page, a half-finished cityscape stared back — an empty skyline.

She stepped closer, her voice gentle. "Here, let me see."

Alma leaned in, her fingers resting lightly on the table's edge. She tapped her nails as she studied Rick's work. He didn't know what he expected her to say — some casual encouragement, maybe a small critique. He prayed she wouldn't laugh, though he wouldn't have blamed her if she did. Instead, she just looked.

The cityscape wasn't working. The buildings stretched awkwardly upward. The shapes were skewed and the perspective felt off — some lines too rigid, others hesitant, like he wasn't sure where they were supposed to lead. The road at the center was meant to pull the eye forward, to create depth. But instead, it felt flat — just two parallel lines at a dead end, failing to tie the scene together. Some sections were overworked, others were unfinished.

She caught it immediately — the misguided lines, not from lack of talent, but from a lack of experience.

"Did El teach you this?" She teased playfully, knowing full well he hadn't.

"Here, let me show you something." She reached for a sheet from a nearby sketch pad. "What do you know about horizon lines and vanishing points?"

During their lessons, El had shown Rick the basics of creating the three-dimensional boxes that disappeared at a single point in the distance. But they had yet to try anything this elaborate. Rick had taken it upon himself to attempt a cityscape, hoping that the studio would provide the lesson.

Rick hesitated. The concept made sense with basic geometric shapes, but he didn't know how to apply the lesson here.

She glanced up at him, a playful smile forming at the corner of her lips, then pulled a pencil from the messy bun piled on her head and sketched a soft horizon line across the page.

Her pencil lifted as she marked a single dot near the center. "This," she said quietly, "is your vanishing point. Everything in the picture eventually leads here."

Rick watched as she leaned in, focused, as if rediscovering something in the act of teaching it. Then, with smooth strokes, she extended two straight lines from the bottom corners of the page, drawing them toward the dot.

"Imagine standing in the middle of a vast desert," Alma explained. "The only thing besides the sand is a long, straight railroad stretching as far as you can see. As you look ahead, the tracks narrow until they disappear into a single point on the horizon. That point where the highway vanishes — that's the vanishing point, where all the lines converge."

She added a series of lines, representing the wooden railroad ties he'd seen before. Each tie shrinking in length, as they approached the vanishing point. "See how they get smaller in the distance? That's perspective. Everything in your image should get smaller in the distance. It's a trick of the mind."

Rick imagined himself standing on that road, the lines pulling his focus forward. He nodded.

His eyes widened as the flat paper seemed to shift — no longer just lines, but a road stretching endlessly into the horizon.

Rick nodded, still absorbing the concept. "So the vanishing point — it's not just about where the lines meet, but where they suggest things could go?"

Alma smiled. "Exactly. It's all about interpretation. If you have ever driven on a long stretch of road," Alma continued, "You can't see beyond the horizon, but you have a sense of the direction it's going."

"Feels a bit like my life right now. I can't see beyond the next moment. I thought I knew where I was headed, but now I have no idea." He thought back to the earlier decision to take the job with Chase.

Alma laughed, "Isn't that the truth?! But what fun would there be in knowing how everything would end? For me, I look at life as an adventure. I assume that one way or another, everything is working in my favor to make me better."

Alma flipped the sheet over that she had been drawing on.

With grace she drew what appeared to be a flowing M and three horizontal, parallel lines, unconnected on the left side. The lines were not symmetrical in length. Each line varied in length, with the shortest one positioned at the top, centered above the second line. The second line was slightly longer than the first, precisely aligned with the third line, which happened to be the longest.

Rick immediately recognized the drawing, it was the same image he saw on her cardboard sign those many weeks ago.

"So the sign didn't say, 'Me'?"

Alma shot him a sideways glance, a smile tugging at her lips.

"You're not the first to think that." Her voice softened. "It's not a word. It's a reminder."

"A reminder of what?" Rick asked, genuinely curious.

Alma let out a quiet laugh. "That gravity sucks."

Rick laughed too, shaking his head. "Gravity sucks?"

"Absolutely." She didn't miss a beat. "At some point, we all find ourselves at the top of the mountain — only to tumble back down. We often feel ourselves at what we consider the bottom, only to find a way to rise back up. This" — she traced the curve of what Rick thought was an M — "is the climb. The rise and fall."

"And these?" Rick tapped the three unfinished lines. "Railroad tracks?" They reminded him of her earlier sketch. He glanced up at her, then nodded toward the lines. "Or the start of an E?"

Alma smiled, but this time it wasn't playful. There was something heavier behind it, like a truth she'd been carrying.

"They're steps," she said quietly. "Never even. Some are short, some long. But if you keep moving, they'll lead you back up — sometimes even higher than where you were before. They change your view of the world. That's been my experience, anyway."

There was a heaviness in her voice, like the words carried more than she was ready to say. Something unspoken tucked behind her easy smile.

"Whether it's life, love, a career — or the stock market — the falls always come faster than the climb," she went on. "One minute you're in the penthouse, the next, the basement — and the elevator's broken."

Alma extended her index finger and mimicked repeatedly pressing an elevator button, as if the frantic jabs could somehow hurry the process along.

"We all do it," she said. "We want to go back up fast. But the elevator doesn't come. So we have to take the stairs. One slow, uneven step at a time. And with each stair, each breath, each climb — you become stronger than the version of you that fell."

Rick listened, but his attention drifted to the sketch of her original sign, the M and the E. He traced one of the letters with his finger, then paused, squinting at the paper. Something pulled at him — familiar.

"There was something else," he murmured, not meaning to say it out loud.

"What's that?" Alma asked.

He shook his head slowly, remembering the speckled dots on the original sign. "Nothing. Just... the first night I saw this sign, there were these specks — they looked like snowflakes, just above the letters."

Alma's expression stayed neutral. It was almost too neutral.

Rick studied Alma's re-creation again. The dots weren't there on her design. The surface was clean, just the letter M and the stairs as she explained them staring back at him.

Weird, he thought. She had been so deliberate with the other elements of the cardboard sign that he was surprised the snowflakes weren't included.

Before Rick could question her further, the lights overhead flickered once, then died. The studio went ink-black. Through the front windows, he could see that the glow from the streetlights had vanished too. Entire buildings across the block were dark.

A power outage. Rare, but not unheard of in the city. This was the third time Rick had experienced one since moving to New York, but it always caught him off guard.

In the darkness, Alma squealed. Rick couldn't see her, but he could picture her grin — the way her eyes squinted when she smiled and her nose scrunched up like a kid on Christmas morning.

"Come on! You're gonna love this," she said, grabbing his hand. Her fingers were small, her skin soft, but her grip was firm.

She tugged him forward, weaving effortlessly through the maze of stools and easels. Rick hesitated, careful not to crash into anything. He could feel her energy pulling him, but his own steps stayed cautious.

"Come on," Alma urged. "You've gotta trust me. Sometimes you need a little faith."

As if on cue, a single canvas near the back of the studio began to glow — a faint, electric-blue pulse emanating from the paint itself. Just enough light for Rick to find his footing.

Trust wasn't something Rick did easily. Faith, even less.

But here he was, following her anyway in the middle of a power outage. Alma led him to the back staircase, ascending quickly, her footsteps hurried but gentle. Rick followed, slower but steady, up to the roof of the warehouse.

When they reached the top, she turned and stretched her arms wide like she was showing off the whole universe. Her hair twirled as she spun like a slowly wound top, staring upward at the heavens.

"Isn't it amazing?"

Rick followed her gaze. The entire skyline was dark — Manhattan did actually sleep. But above them, the sky twinkled with life. He had never seen such a dazzling display of the night sky in New York. On most nights, the light pollution was far too bright to even see the faintest twinkle.

Millions of stars scattered across the night like specks of paint on an inky black canvas, clear and sharp, as if the city had pulled back the curtains just for this moment.

It reminded him of the Western nights of his childhood — how small he used to feel beneath all that sky, and yet somehow more significant, like he belonged to something bigger. But here, in the middle of the city, it felt almost impossible.

There they stood, in the heart of Manhattan, discovering the most magical painting of them all. It was a cosmos of possibility, finally visible because everything else had gone dark. The irony wasn't lost on Rick. Sometimes, you had to lose the light to finally see.

As his eyes adjusted to the quiet brilliance above, he paused — not because of the stars, but because of the soft silhouette beside him.

The quarter moon cast just enough light to reveal her face, and for the first time, he saw them clearly. The snowflakes, the speckles, the dots — whatever they were — on Alma's original cardboard sign had been right in front of him all along. He'd been so focused on the distant horizon of his own career that he had missed them altogether.

Though his future was out of focus, the current moment became clear.

Without thinking, he reached out, his fingers gently tracing a line between each freckle on her cheek, then over the bridge of her nose and to the other side. In his mind, he began to connect the dots of his own life — the highs, the lows, the events, and mostly the decisions that had brought him to this moment.

"Little miracles," Alma said, referencing the freckles on her face. "My grandmother said we all collect them. She said I just collected mine on my cheeks for the world to see. She said our experiences are drawn on all of us."

Alma reached up, placing her hand behind Rick's head and pulling him close. In an instant, Rick realized this might just be the miracle he'd been hoping for. In a single night, he landed what was once his dream job — and at the same time, discovered the potential of an amazing new relationship.

Armed with a new perspective, both smiled as the lights over Manhattan woke up.

The only problem was, he hadn't told Alma he'd decided to take the job with Chase.

CHAPTER 13

ADDING COLOR TO THE CANVAS

It was hard to believe — more than six months had passed since Rick first met El and Alma. In that time, his life had shifted in ways he never expected. A new role was waiting — working alongside Chase Mercer, a rare opportunity that stirred both excitement and unease. He was ready. But part of him didn't want to leave the studio behind.

Zivot had become more than a place to practice his craft. With the tools of the studio in hand, a growing relationship with Alma, a life mentor in El, and a circle of new friends, Rick wasn't just rebuilding his life — he was redesigning it.

He'd found harmony — not by avoiding discomfort, but by walking through it. And Alma — who once wandered, never staying in one place too long — had found something steadier in him. In their time together, she felt less like a wanderer and more like someone learning how to stay.

Through his apprenticeship, Rick had committed himself to the lessons of both Alma and El. Week by week, his journey unfolded — not just in technique, but in reflection and growth.

He'd even been invited to join the teaching team at Zivot. Though he'd never claim mastery, he was learning — developing, helping others discover their own voice.

Before his led his first class, El offered a quiet reminder. "You don't have to be a master artist, Rick," he said. "Zivot is the real teacher." Rick's role wasn't to deliver answers — it was to create space. A place for others to try, to notice, to grow.

"You have to let them 'fail,' Rick," El added. But Rick knew El didn't mean failure in the conventional sense. Instead, El encouraged him to provide students with a foundation of knowledge and then step back — to let them explore, experiment, and grow, even when their lines didn't turn out as planned.

In this space of exploration, Rick witnessed countless moments of brilliance. Time and again, unexpected breakthroughs emerged from what seemed like beautiful, catastrophic failures — proving the studio itself was the greatest teacher of all.

To Rick, every untouched canvas became a symbol of limitless potential, beckoning him to explore the uncharted territories of his creativity. He had grown to appreciate the power of taking up a new canvas and the sacrifice that was required to start anew. He longed to discover the potential within the blank and empty space. He found himself often staring into blank spaces, caught between the mystery and imagination of what might lay dormant on the new and pristine surface.

He was learning to capture the creative spark that could be found within a single point, and the power contained in the artist with the courage to pick up the pen and pull that line forward to discover its full potential. He understood that every stroke of the pen had the power to bring thoughts to life, transforming a pristine surface into a visual masterpiece.

Guided by a newfound appreciation for the artist's journey, Rick began to understand that creating was not simply a task but a sacred act of courage and vulnerability.

Each day, he took deliberate time to create, set an objective, and ensure it aligned with his weekly goal. This ritual wasn't just a habit — it was his way of living out one of El's core lessons: **L.I.N.E.—Live Intentionally. No Excuses.**

Rick was having fun, more fun than he'd had in years. The blank canvas was no longer an intimidating expanse but a playground of endless possibilities. Each day, when the day's lessons ended, Rick would often work late into the night, refining his own skills or reviewing the lessons he would need to teach the following day. Other times, he would work side by side with Alma, taking turns drawing lines, then adding to what the other had just created. Life became a collaborative process.

Tonight, however, he was alone. It was just him, his pen, and a piece of artboard. Rick stood back, examining his blank canvas.

The more he learned, the more he worked; and the more he worked, the more he realized how easy it was to become fixated on a project.

He had been so intently focused that he found himself hunched above the surface for hours, paying attention to every detail. Each individual stroke of the pen seemed to contort his body into an uncomfortable position. Ergonomics were completely out the window as he strived for mastery. His neck ached and his eyes were strained.

"You're chasing the unattainable, Rick." El's words echoed in Rick's mind, a lesson from an earlier time in his apprenticeship.

"That's got to be good for tonight," Rick said aloud to no one in particular. The studio was silent — El had left hours ago, and Alma had gone home not long after, promising to meet him in the morning. It was just Rick and the building now, but the racks of paintings and line work seemed to hear him as they hummed quietly in the stillness.

After cleaning up and putting away his supplies, he could have sworn that the vibrant colors of the various artists' works grew just a little brighter as he shut off the lights and exited the building. They then hummed with an electric-blue glow as if to say goodbye.

Not thinking any more of it, he began closing the door to Zivot Studio and felt a single wet drop hit his forehead and then another. He had been so intently focused on his work that he didn't realize that it was raining outside.

"I swear the rain never stops in this city." Rick stood outside, his gaze fixed on the pouring rain. As heavy droplets pelted his face, he couldn't help but reflect on the constant showers that plagued the city. This autumn's rainfall seemed unusually heavy. Shielding his eyes, Rick pulled his trusty black hoodie high onto his head, seeking refuge from the downpour that fell like a wall of water. However, he knew he would be soaked to the bone in no time.

Rick fumbled in his pocket and retrieved a key chain. On it was a single well-worn key. The once shiny brass had faded over the years, bearing witness to time's passage. Holding it between his thumb and forefinger, Rick felt an overwhelming sense of honor. It was just a few nights ago that El had given him this key, entrusting him with the responsibility of locking up the studio at night when neither he nor Alma was available.

In the grand scheme of things, Rick hadn't known El for long. Yet, he was deeply touched that El had chosen him for such an important task. Perhaps El felt there was no other option. Unlike El and Alma, who were early birds, Rick preferred starting his day later, taking breaks in the afternoon and staying late into the night. When El wasn't around, it was usually Alma who locked up. But with her tendency to wander, there were nights where Rick had no choice but to leave with the building left unlocked. In those instances, Rick would leave with a lingering guilt weighing on him.

Maybe it happened one too many times, making El fearful that one of the more unsavory characters of the neighborhood might wander in. After gently pushing the door completely shut, Rick inserted the key into the deadbolt, turning it clockwise until the latch engaged. Giving the door a final tug to confirm it was secure, he turned to cross the street.

The rain may have been relentless, but Rick's commitment to the studio and his newfound responsibility burned bright within him.

Rick took two steps across the sidewalk, then a third, stepping onto the asphalt. On his fourth step, the world went black — pitch black, blending into the rain-soaked night sky. The hoodie he'd pulled forward to shield himself from the downpour blocked his view of everything ahead, leaving him unaware of the headlights cutting through the storm until it was too late.

The blare of a horn and the screech of tires shattered the rain-soaked night. Rick barely had time to process the sound before the impact sent him hurtling through the air, his body crashing onto the wet, unforgiving pavement. The faint clink of the well-worn key slipping from his fingers was lost in the storm. Finally, he registered the dull thud of his head hitting the asphalt before unconsciousness swept over him, dragging him into an inky black void where the world ceased to exist.

For the next few days, Rick lost all sense of time, unaware of how long had passed since the night of the accident. Like having been lost in a deep sleep, he was unaware of anything around him. Though the world continued at the same bustling pace that you would expect in New York, to Rick it was motionless, just as his body was.

It wasn't until he was awakened by awful pulsing sounds, circling around him in a counterclockwise rhythm, that he knew something was wrong. The sound started as a jackhammer, then shifted — to something like a combination of bending, buzzing, clicking, and intermittent beeps. The noise was relentless, dull but loud, as though muffled by thick earplugs. He thought he could feel something lodged in his ears, but the sensation was distant, uncertain, like the rest of him.

The faint chill of the wind brushed his face again, stirring enough awareness for the words to escape his lips, "Where am I?"

Rick's body throbbed. He tried to sit up, but his shoulders were pinned down, two walls on either side pushed his arms against his body. Groaning, his back ached as it pressed against a cold, hard table.

Confused, he worked to open his eyes. He saw a thin black line just inches from his face. As his eyes adjusted, he realized it was the seam between a yellowed, round, plastic tube surrounding him.

"Rick. Hey, Rick, I'm going to need you to hold still for a few more minutes." The buzzing and whirring had stopped and a voice echoed from a speaker inside the tube. Rick couldn't see anyone, but he got the visual impression that the mysterious, disembodied voice belonged to someone outside of the tube, coming from a microphone.

"Now just hold still. You're in the hospital and we're just finishing your MRI."

The hospital? MRI? What had happened? As he processed the words, he caught the whiff of a stale sanitary cleanser and then the unmistakable smell of alcohol swabs.

This was really happening. Rick felt the slightly uncomfortable pinch of an IV in his left hand.

Rick had little memory of the events that had brought him to this point. He vaguely remembered leaving the studio, a heavy rain, and hitting his head — but other than that, he had no memory of how he got there. He was just grateful to be coherent. When he had first awakened, confused about where he was, he thought he might be dead.

Then all at once, he became intensely aware of a pain that engulfed his body. Everything hurt, but especially his head. It was intense and relentless. His headache began as a deep, pulsating ache, as if his head was being squeezed from within. The pressure grew steadily, radiating out from the center of his skull. The pain synchronized with the metallic whirring of the MRI machine. But soon the rhythmic pain came to a close.

Rick let out a scream. He couldn't help it. The pain was unlike anything he had ever felt before.

The attending staff were quick to respond. Still trapped in the MRI tube, Rick didn't see the nurse and doctor push fluid into his IV, but he suddenly felt his body become warm and a strange taste entered his mouth. It was a faint metallic taste that began to coat his tongue as the medication was pushed into his bloodstream.

The cool sting of medication coursed through his veins, pulling him under. Like the MRI tube, sleep swallowed him whole, dragging him into an indistinct void. The whirring of the MRI faded into nothingness, replaced by a heavy stillness.

Time passed in meaningless flashes. Minutes turned to hours and hours to days. When the sedation lightened, Rick floated in and out of awareness, tethered only by brief sensations or momentary awareness. Dim light stabbed at his fluttering eyelids, blinding him even through the haze. Muffled voices swirled around him, their words just out of reach. Alma's voice stood out at times, soft and steady, though it quickly dissolved before he could engage with it.

In fleeting moments of clarity, he became aware of other sensations — a chair scraping softly against the floor, the shuffle of footsteps coming and going. Suddenly, a hand brushed against his own, warm, soft and gentle, but it lingered for only a moment. Was it real? Or another fragment of a dream? He couldn't be sure, nor could he respond.

The world was a haze — a soft, shifting shadow of reality that ebbed and flowed with his fragile consciousness. Alma and Fernando lingered quietly in the room, their presence a silent sentinel in case he stirred. For now, though, there was nothing to do but wait.

Through the veiled fog of a state between consciousness and unconsciousness, a voice broke through — a familiar one. The voice called to him.

"Rick? Rick, are you awake?"

The sound was soft yet distinct, cutting through the murky void like a lifeline. Rick stirred faintly, confusion threading through his fragmented awareness. That voice... it couldn't be real, but it was.

Rick forced his eyes open. It was his friend and mentor calling him. "El? Is that you?" Rick had difficulty getting his eyes to focus. Everything was blurry. He thought it was El, but Rick swore that he looked different.

"Yes, Rick, it's me. I'm so glad you are awake. I need your help."

As Rick processed the request, he found it strange. Strange that El was asking him to immediately help, just as he awoke in the hospital.

"Come with me! I need help with a collection." El said excitedly.

"Okay, I just need them to come and unhook me..." Rick's words trailed off. He reached for the IV's, oxygen and heart-monitoring leads that he remembered being on his body during the MRI, but curiously, they were already disconnected. To his surprise, he was in his regular clothes and his body felt fine. In fact, it felt better than he had recalled in years. The only thing that felt off were his eyes. He rubbed them again, but they were no better. Everything seemed a bit out of focus.

Feeling spry, Rick swung his legs over the side of the bed and stood with surprising ease. No stiffness, no aches — just effortless movement. He felt light, almost weightless, as he followed El toward the door.

As they stepped into the hallway, Rick caught sight of Alma and Fernando seated in the waiting area. Alma was hunched forward, her hands clasped tightly in her lap. Her voice cracked as she spoke.

"I'm so worried about him, Fernando. I can't believe this is happening. First El... now Rick. It's more than I can take."

Rick stopped in his tracks. What did she mean — first El?

He could hear every word she said — but more than that, he could feel her thoughts. Communication had never been more clear: *This isn't fair. Not again. I finally let someone in... and now I'm losing him too.*

She was angry. Hurt. Frightened. He stepped closer. "Alma, I'm okay," he said gently. "I'm right here."

But there was no response. He waved a hand in front of her face. Nothing.

He reached out to touch her shoulder, but his hand passed through her like fog.

A cold realization hit him in the chest. He turned, slowly, as if pulled by some invisible thread.

There — back in the hospital room — was a figure lying in the bed. Pale, still, and flat.

Rick took a step closer, staring at the face of the body in the bed. It was him.

His body, unmoving except a faint breath beneath the thin hospital blanket.

The weight of the moment grew.

He turned to El, panic rising in his voice. "Am I..." But the words died on his lips.

Suddenly his eyes had clarity. Complete and clear clarity. It was El, but not the El who had mentored him. He was young and active.

"El, is that really you? Am I dead?"

"It's me, Rick." El wore the same crazy, paint-splattered, mad-scientist-inspired lab coat he always had. But that didn't seem to be enough for Rick. As if to put an exclamation mark on the conversation, El leaned in close and the wrinkles in his face were gone, his skin considerably younger. He then pulled up the sleeve of his lab coat to reveal the outline of a bold-lettered tattoo. It was a single line of text that ran the length of his outer forearm, directly over the bone, it read...

"Learn the rules like a pro, so you can break them like an artist."
– Pablo Picasso

Rick recognized it immediately, but it was now unmistakably fresh. It appeared to have been newly inked, sharp and vibrant, and it glowed a cool electric blue.

"Sorry, Rick. We're breaking a few rules with this one. You're not dead, but the Great Creator insisted that you be here. He brought you here."

The next thing Rick knew, they were standing back in Zivot Studio. Every emotion Rick had ever experienced in the studio hit him all at once. He could smell waffles, linseed oil, ink, and sandalwood. He remembered the confusion of his first lesson, accepting the apprenticeship, and every other lesson he had been taught. He recalled his first mistake with the nib, and the ink splatter and semi-straight line that looked like an italicized i.

"What are we doing here, El? What is this?"

"You don't remember the studio? Man, that car must have hit you hard!" El laughed.

As El said it, Rick remembered being hit by a car in the rain. He remembered locking up the shop, the screeching tires as the speeding vehicle attempted to avoid hitting him, and the sound of the worn brass key as it hit the pavement. That was just before everything went dark.

"I need your help, Rick. I need your help with my final collection." El's eyes grew big as he held out his arms.

"Your collection?"

Rick looked around the room and noticed that the warehouse shelves were now completely empty. There were no glowing canvases on the rack. Instead, there were countless stacks of canvases wrapped neatly in brown parchment, carefully secured with brown twine, meticulously tied with an impeccably knotted bow.

"Yes," El said, gesturing to the wrapped packages. "It's our last lesson, and it's an important one. As part of your apprenticeship, you had the opportunity to attend our underground art exhibit, you saw the displays, and now I get to share my collection with you. My life's collection of work."

Once again confused, Rick looked at him blankly. His head hurt, but he remembered the exhibit and the displays. "What's the difference between an exhibit, an installation, a display, and a collection?"

"Great question!" El's eyes grew big again.

"Let's begin with displays," El said, his voice bubbling with enthusiasm. "Imagine walking into a museum or gallery, where a painting is on display and sculptures stand tall, carefully arranged for all to admire. These displays can be found in museums, schools, and even hotels, a way to showcase specific pieces. The items on display are usually just pieces of a larger work. If you compare that to life, it might be a single day taken from a lifetime out of maybe seventy-five or a hundred years. It offers a glimpse into a larger window."

"And exhibits?" Rick asked.

El continued his explanation, going deeper.

"But exhibits — ah, I love exhibits. These are special events where a group of art pieces, sometimes from multiple artists, are brought together, weaving a narrative, telling a story around a common theme or idea. Just like the underground art showcase we organized, exhibits immerse you in a world of creativity and wonder. They extend beyond a single piece — they're designed to challenge people, to make us think and question."

As Rick's fascination grew, El moved on to art collections.

"A collection, on the other hand, is more personal. It's a kind of treasure trove, Rick — one that reflects an individual's tastes and interests. A collection might consist of paintings from a single artist or sculptures tied to a particular era. These collections tell stories too — revealing the passions and curiosities of the people or institutions who gather them."

El paused for a moment, then leaned in.

"But beyond galleries and the walls that house them, there's something deeper. Each of us has been placed on this earth to create our own work of art."

He tapped the table lightly as he spoke. "We're all given a timeline. We're handed different tools. We live with different perspectives, challenges, and desires. Some of us are acutely aware of the work we're creating. Others are just trying to survive. But inside every life, we make our mark. As long as there's space left in our timeline, we have access to an unlimited number of canvases to design, draw, and doodle. Every decision, every action — even inaction — is inked into our life's work. Our personal collection."

But it was El's final metaphor — an installation — that captured Rick's imagination.

El's voice took on a mesmerizing tone.

"Now, picture an art installation, Rick. It's no ordinary artwork; it's immersive. A full-sensory experience that transcends boundaries. You step into a room, and the entire space becomes part of the piece — sculptures, lights, sound, video — all working together to stir emotion and provoke thought."

Rick sat quietly, letting the idea sink in.

"So, I was right. The apprenticeship was never really about art, was it?"

El smiled.

"The apprenticeship we all participate in is never really about art."

He looked Rick in the eye.

"Our apprenticeship is life. It includes every mark we make — the good, the bad, the unintentional. We're all creating together. And in the end, we're part of one giant, cosmic art installation."

El's voice resonated with hope and optimism. "Imagine what that moment must have been like, being invited to participate in the creation of an art installation that spans the cosmos. We have a priceless opportunity to create alongside the universe. Our apprenticeship offers us a palette of emotions — love, hate, anger, fear, hope, and kindness — all tailored to our needs. Within this masterpiece, we contribute our own unique design, shaping the ever-evolving image."

Rick felt a surge of inspiration and newfound clarity. The world of art, the art of life, had opened up before him — a realm of self-discovery and personal growth. He now appreciated more than ever the daily choices he made, understanding how each response to circumstances beyond his control added an element to his personal creation. He realized how every line he walked had the potential to branch into a new creative element. He appreciated the power to deliberately design, detail, and decide to create a work that could be part of the great installation of the cosmos.

"But what do you need from me, El? Why am I here?"

Tears welled in the eyes of Rick's mentor — not tears of sadness, but of profound gratitude for a life well-lived. They were also tears of hope — a hope that Rick would accept El's final request.

Rick repeated the questions, "But what do you need from me, El? Why am I here?"

El didn't answer right away. He walked over to one of the neatly wrapped canvases in the studio. Rick watched in awe as El untied the bow. The paper fell, and to his astonishment, the canvas lifted into the air as if by magic. One by one, El repeated the process, and each canvas gracefully floated, effortlessly lining up, rising into place along a small stretch of cosmic time. Rick was witnessing the unfolding of El's life.

Rick marveled at the linear representations of El's journey. This wasn't just any line — it was El's storyline. Every image began on the canvas as a single point, a spark of creation. Rick was mesmerized as he watched an unseen ink nib glide across the surface, leaving behind inky black, white, and grayscale lines. Each line eventually came to an end, only to branch out or continue onto a new canvas, revealing a fresh visual. These were individual branching plotlines, intricately woven into a broader, unified story.

But the magic didn't stop there. The lines shimmered, pulsating with energy before bursting into vibrant, vivid colors. They lifted off the canvas, transforming into living, three-dimensional scenes that moved with purpose. Events unfolded like chapters in a book, blending seamlessly from one moment to the next. Together, they created a tapestry of interconnected stories — rich with meaning and connection. Yet, through it all, every line remained visible and clear, anchoring the narrative for the observer.

As Rick leaned into the experience, the perspective shifted. The canvases zoomed outward, and suddenly, he wasn't just watching El's story — he was seeing the intricate web of paths that had led to this moment. Every step, every choice, every turn was connected, forming an expansive network of overlapping lines. Each path sparkled with light, hinting at moments of triumph, heartbreak, and discovery. He could see how El's life intertwined with others, how one event sparked a ripple that touched countless lives.

It began with El's early life. A single line bloomed into the story of his parents' love, the warmth of their embrace, and the moment of El's first breath and first smile. It continued as he crawled. He watched as that line ended, branching into another — his first wobbly steps, marked by dashed lines of repeated falls, until the line steadied and transformed into the joyful path of a run.

Rick's gaze followed as the canvas shifted, revealing pivotal moments in El's life. He watched El's family migrate to the United States, their lines blazing brightly as they left everything behind in search of a better world. Shapes morphed fluidly before his eyes — a circle became the wheels of a bicycle, then the silhouette of a car, each evolution marking a milestone in El's growth.

The perspective expanded again, the canvas shifting like a camera panning through time. The car's outline transformed into a tank, representing El's decision to enlist. Rick saw a military front line as El's adventures intersected with countless others — the soldiers he fought beside, some of their paths ending abruptly, while others continued onward.

Amid the chaos of war, Rick saw another line appear — a woman's. It carried a grace and resilience that contrasted with El's, yet complemented it perfectly. Their lines wove together with vibrant energy, intertwining as love blossomed between them. Their shared journey unfolded — full of perseverance, laughter, and hope, even when their lines of communication wavered.

The perspective shifted again, pulling Rick further outward. Millions of points and lines formed a shimmering constellation of El's decisions, each connected to another in ways Rick couldn't fully grasp. The lines pulsed with light, illustrating growth, resilience, and the triumph of the human spirit. Negative moments and immense challenges were overshadowed by the brilliance of learning, love, and success.

But as the images slowed, Rick felt a pang of unease. A scene materialized, one he wished he could forget. A homeless man held a blank canvas, his eyes pleading with a businessman who walked past him without a second glance. Rick's stomach twisted — it was him. Not the night he first met El, but long before.

The canvas replayed forgotten moments. Time after time, El had appeared in Rick's life, standing on the periphery, unnoticed or outright ignored. Rick watched himself hurry past, consumed by his own world. The lines of their lives only truly intersected the day after Rick's layoff, when pain and humility finally opened his eyes to a new opportunity.

The canvas zoomed out once more, revealing a breathtaking view of all the paths that had converged to bring them here. Rick saw how his journey had become part of something far greater — a single thread woven into a vast, interconnected tapestry. At the center of this cosmic canvas was an outlined silhouette of Rick and El standing side by side, watching the masterpiece of El's life unfold.

Unlike the vibrant, colorful scenes before it, this image was rendered in stark black-and-white line work, raw and incomplete. It seemed to hold a quiet promise, as if the image were still unfolding, waiting for the final touch.

In that final moment, El turned to Rick. "Rick, I need your help. My work here is nearly done, but I believe yours is just beginning. I'd like you to take the studio to teach others. I need you to help them see the power of a line, the fact that they and they alone control the path that their line will travel."

Rick's eyes now welled with tears. "I can't, El. I'm not an artist. You haven't even taught me to paint. All I have is a basic understanding of line work."

El's eyes seemed to reflect the cosmic stardust that surrounded them, the backdrop an image that could only have been designed by the Great Creator. "Rick, my boy, our lessons never end. There is much you will experience and much you will be taught, but you have everything that you need right now to begin to teach others. You have the one piece of knowledge that many have not acquired. You need to share it with them," he paused.

Taking a deep breath, El continued, "Every man, woman, and child needs to know that they control the pen, but they must have the courage to draw up the ink and control the line. They can make corrections along the way and they can start again at any time, adding a new image to their collection."

What could Rick say to that? The gravity of El's request weighed on him — a heavy burden, a tap on the shoulder from a greater power he had been asked to carry. He certainly had questions, but he knew this moment had been created as a crossroads for his personal discovery.

It was an opportunity for Rick to add to his own collection and allow El to close out his masterpiece, knowing that his legacy would live on.

El held out the deed to Zivot Studio. Rick looked into El's eyes. "Are you sure I'm ready for this?"

El nodded, "The color and the paint come easy once you understand the power of a line. Masterpieces were never meant to be created with a single medium. Ink, charcoal, pencil, paint — they all add different properties and values to our work. When we collaborate with others, we allow them to assist us in creating an imaginative and colorful work of art. That's what I'm asking of you, Rick." Tears welled in El's eyes.

"Collaborators bring techniques that you haven't yet mastered. Together, we learn to work in color, adding variety in all its different shades. We discover reds full of passion and anger, blues of sadness, yellows of joy — each hue, shade, and tone imaginable.

There are certainly times when the work is solely the responsibility of the one holding the canvas, but there is an electricity and excitement that can only be generated when creative forces join together — when lines intersect. It happens when we surround ourselves with other amazing artists. It happens when we mentor others who haven't yet learned the lessons we have, but it all starts with the power of a line."

Tears danced down the face of both men now. Once again, El held out the deed to Zivot Studio. He motioned for Rick to take it, along with a precisely balanced ink pen.

Rick smiled, took the deed, and signed on the dotted line, accepting the great responsibility he had been given.

As he lifted the pen from the deed, Rick looked up to the mural of El's life. With Rick's signature, the last canvas began to fill with bright, vibrant, and painted colors. It was no longer a flat, one-dimensional canvas. It was El's completed masterpiece, and Rick had been a part of it.

In that moment, as the canvases hovered in the air, full of color, Rick realized the profound impact one person's life could have on others.

With a serene smile, El delivered the final lesson. "You see, Rick, we guide the lines of our lives, but it's the intersections with others — their paths, their stories — that add texture, vibrancy, and depth to our canvas. Thank you, Rick, for what you've added to mine."

And just like that, El was gone, vanishing into the ether. The experience, however, was etched into Rick's soul as vividly as a masterful stroke on a blank canvas.

Rick watched in awe as every canvas, every star, and every line in the cosmic gallery dissolved into an infinite blackness. Where did it all go? he wondered, the thought lingering as the emptiness enveloped him. Moments later, he jolted awake, his head heavy and his throat raw from the dry hospital oxygen. Blinking against the harsh light, his vision adjusted to the sterile room, and his eyes landed on Alma, sitting quietly by his side.

"Are you okay?" Rick rasped, his voice barely above a whisper.

Alma jumped, startled by the sound. Her eyes widened in disbelief. "Oh my gosh, Rick, you're awake!" She leaned in to embrace him, her tears slipping onto his cheeks. "I'm okay, but Rick..." her voice broke. "There's something I need to tell you. It's bad news — hard to hear."

Rick closed his eyes for a moment, steadying himself. When he spoke, his voice carried a calmness that surprised them both. "It's okay, Alma. I know. El's line ended. His masterpiece is complete."

Alma froze, staring at him in disbelief. "You know?" she asked, incredulously.

Rick swallowed hard, the dryness in his throat clawing at him. He longed to share what had happened — the vivid, otherworldly encounter with El — but the question loomed: Would she believe him? And if not, how would she react when she learned that El had entrusted Rick with the future of the studio?

Before he could speak, a buzz from the nightstand cut through the quiet.

Alma handed him his phone. One new message from Chase:

> *I tried calling last week. Just heard about the accident.*
> *The partners pulled the offer — figured you'd be out for a while.*
> *Hope you bounce back quickly.*

Rick read it once. Then again. No reaction. No reply.

He set the phone down like it was already in the past.

Whatever Chase thought he took away, he didn't.

Rick had seen the bigger picture, and now he knew — Chase had nothing to do with it.

CHAPTER 14

CELEBRATION OF LIFE

The world had kept moving while Rick lay still, unconscious in a hospital bed — days of life unfolding without him. Alma shared every detail he had missed while he was sedated after the injury — the phone call she received, the first time she saw him lying unconscious and bruised on the gurney. She recounted current events, snippets of news, and conversations at the studio. They talked for hours, her voice filling in the gaps of his lost time. For Alma, the waiting felt like an eternity, each moment stretched by fear and uncertainty. For Rick, waking up felt like no time had passed at all — as if the accident and recovery had occurred in an instant while he took a deep nap.

Time, Rick thought, had always been a fickle keeper of experiences — dragging slowly when he anticipated something exciting and racing ahead during life's most magical moments. The only traces it ever left behind were the precious memories he held on to; the passing of time took everything else with it. Without memories, time might have never existed. But in this case, time had done him a favor, shielding him from the memories of the countless tubes and machines that once surrounded him. He couldn't have been more grateful. Though he was sore, the most significant pain had been left in the past.

Alma was both grateful for Rick's safe recovery and intrigued by his story of an out-of-body experience with El. She even admitted, with a touch of envy, that she had always wondered what the other side might be like. Rick's vivid description sounded like everything she had hoped for, leaving her with no question about his sincerity. And if any doubt had existed, his retelling of her and Fernando's hallway conversation, word for word, erased it. There was no way he could have overheard them otherwise.

The accident had occurred ten days ago. After spending seven days in the hospital and three days adjusting to life post-release, Rick and Alma were on their way to the studio to bid farewell to their dear friend and mentor. Rick understood the road ahead would be long, filled with rehabilitation, follow-up appointments, and challenges. Yet, the idea of a new canvas — both literal and figurative — sparked hope. He was eager to see what adventures the future might hold for him and Alma.

Fernando and the rest of the studio had been incredible. Aware that Rick was still healing, they insisted he and Alma focus on rest. They took care of everything — the studio's upkeep, the arrangements, the flowers, and every detail for the day. True to El's wishes, the celebration of life was to be held at Zivot, among his closest friends, in the glow of the space that had inspired so much creativity.

Though Rick's apartment was normally within walking distance of the studio, they opted for a rideshare. Minutes later, they arrived at Zivot Studio, where a line of people from all walks of life stretched out the door, waiting to pay their respects to the legendary artist and mentor. Rick couldn't help but wonder just how many lives El had touched.

As they stepped out of the vehicle and exchanged pleasantries with the driver, Fernando greeted them warmly and gently guided Rick and Alma past the waiting crowd and into the studio.

Inside, the atmosphere was one of reflection and gratitude — an ideal celebration of life with unique touches that could only have come from El. The expansive studio, once a bustling hub of creativity, had been transformed into a makeshift chapel for the funeral. Heavy drapes, used for exhibitions, partitioned the warehouse into intimate spaces, guiding visitors through a carefully curated path that celebrated El's life and work before opening into a chapel-like setting for the service itself.

Four distinct stations greeted visitors before they approached the room where El's casket rested. True to his vision and commitment to Zivot, El had gone so far as to design the experience as his last gift to those kind enough to pay their respects — a final effort to leave the world better than he had found it.

As patrons entered the building, they were greeted by El's final exhibit, simply titled "Linework." On the outer perimeter of the studio, a framed note hung before the first piece. Written in El's unmistakable handwriting, it carried a simple yet profound message:

Curator's Note

What follows are not original pieces. I have simply curated the lines I found in the artistry of your lives. I am not the creator but the curator of your lessons. Thank you!

– El

The familiar script felt deeply personal, as though El himself were standing beside each visitor, guiding them through the final masterpiece.

Rick wiped a tear from Alma's cheek as she read the note aloud, then brushed away his own. The humility of their mentor's final words resonated.

As they moved through the exhibit, Rick recognized many of the lines El had shared with him over the course of their friendship. The fine line of interpretation was a reminder to interpret events in a way that empowered rather than constrained. A timeline depicted the idea that every end was a new beginning. The line of scrimmage, horizon lines, and fault lines were all there, each representing their unique lessons. Perspective lines illustrated the same event viewed from multiple vantage points, while leading lines guided the viewer's eye to focal points on the canvas.

The most intricate piece was a single, continuous line forming the shape of a human ear — a powerful representation of the complexities in the lines of communication. Nearby, Rick saw his own imperfect line of accountability, complete with its ink-spotted blemish above the italicized i. This time, the line was underlined by a continuous path that occasionally jagged upward or downward before correcting itself. It took Rick a moment to recognize it as the line of adaptation — a reflection of the course corrections needed on our journey.

Finally, Rick reached the last display. It was El's canvas — the one Rick had originally purchased. Once blank, it now bore the same thick black line that had first captured his attention, demonstrating the power of simplicity. But this time, there were two lines, both thick and bold.

"I don't understand," Rick said, turning to Alma. "Have you seen this before?"

"No," she replied, holding his hand. They both lingered, oblivious to the line of people waiting behind them. Rick's mind raced. Had he forgotten this lesson?

Fernando approached, sensing their confusion. Leaning in just enough for them to hear, he said with a steady voice, "That's the line of intention."

"But why are there two?" Rick asked.

Fernando smiled knowingly. "Ah, the second line is the front line."

Rick immediately recalled El's story about his friend delivering supplies to the front lines during the war — the critical role those lines played in any battle.

Fernando's voice softened. "El wanted to remind us all that leading with intent means stepping up to those critical lines. The perceived dangers, the challenges — we face them head-on when we fully commit to living intentionally. Both lines are bold, Rick, just as you'll need to be as you step forward to lead the studio."

Fernando stepped back, allowing Rick and Alma to continue their journey to pay respects to El. Along the way, they passed three tattoo stations set up by artists who, at one point or another, had been mentored by El. Each station had a sign-up sheet where visitors could register for a free fine-line tattoo, choosing from any of the lines on display in the exhibit. The tattoos were performed with a single needle, intentionally delicate and elegant. Though these tattoos could be quickly done, they also served as lasting reminders of lessons learned.

"Wow," Rick murmured, his eyes widening as he saw the length of the sign-up list.

One of the artists caught his reaction and grinned. "Yep, we'll happily be here all day," she said with a warm smile.

A few feet farther, Rick and Alma rounded a curtained partition and found themselves before El's casket. The lid was closed. El had told Fernando he didn't want to be remembered as lifeless — his goal had always been to make an impact, even in death. With the lid closed, the casket itself made that statement on his behalf.

The casket was a masterpiece, designed to look as though it had been carved from a single hollowed-out tree. Intricate murals, each representing moments from El's life, adorned its surface, all tied together by various lines. In some sections, the wood retained the texture of bark, with deep grooves reinforcing the illusion of weathered, natural beauty. The carvings were rendered in stunning three-dimensional detail, so precise that Rick couldn't tell if they had been painted, stained, or a combination of both. The surface had an almost ceramic-like smoothness, blending earthy warmth with artistic sophistication.

As Rick studied the craftsmanship, he couldn't shake the feeling that he'd seen something similar before. It reminded him of the themed carvings you might find at the entrance to an iconic amusement-park ride — artistic, immersive, and brimming with story. His gaze fell on one particular carving — a roller coaster. Cartoon-like figures formed a line of eager riders waiting to board. Rick couldn't resist; he reached out and traced the steep incline of the track with his fingers, following it down the sharp descent and over the rolling hills. He noticed a pattern — each drop was met with a rise, a symbolic reminder of the rewards that come after weathering life's falls.

The carvings wrapped around every side of the casket, each side telling a story. On the lid, words had been etched in bold, flowing letters:

Live, Love, Lead, and Learn with Intention. No Excuses.

At the foot of the casket, Rick spotted a new symbol — a horizontal number eight, the unmistakable sign of infinite potential. It was a line he had yet to explore, but its meaning struck him instantly.

Tears streamed freely down Rick and Alma's faces — not from sadness, but from sheer gratitude. The casket wasn't just a farewell; it was a final lesson, a testament to El's artistry and the life he lived with such purpose.

Rick lingered, captivated by the details, but Alma tugged gently at his hand. "Come on," she whispered softly. There were others waiting for their turn to honor El's life and legacy.

They moved on to the final part of the experience, fulfilling one of El's last wishes. A long white table stood in the center of the room, covered with chisel-tipped felt markers and stacks of plain 4- x 6-inch pieces of artboard. Each guest was asked to draw a single line in a form of their choosing. On the back, they were to write an interpretation of their line and make a promise to share it with someone who either needed or embodied the spirit of that line.

This simple act was evidence that El's lessons would carry on.

Finally, Rick and Alma made their way to an open area still within view of the casket. It was where the butcher-block tables and chairs had once stood, now cleared to make space for attendees. There were no chairs — this would be a standing-room-only event. The room was already packed, so they positioned themselves near the front, where a microphone had been set up.

For the next thirty minutes or so, Rick and Alma mingled, exchanging small talk and hearing stories of how others had met El and their experiences at the studio. Each story added another layer to their understanding of El.

Then Fernando, ever the leader, took charge and ensured everyone made it inside the building. If he had waited, the lines outside could have stretched on for hours. Instead, he took it upon himself to shepherd the attendees into the studio, in preparation for the service.

Once everyone was in place, Fernando stepped to the front, turned on the microphone, and gestured for Rick to join him. Rick had been asked to conduct the event.

Rick stood there, glancing at his watch. The room fell silent as everyone watched him, confusion flickering across their faces as he simply waited, letting the seconds tick by. Finally, the minute hand shifted.

11:11
Live Intentionally. No Excuses.

"El was insistent that we start at 11:11," Rick said, breaking the silence. "What can I say? He loved his lines." The room erupted in laughter as they realized the time was marked by four perfectly straight lines.

As the laughter subsided, Rick took a moment to absorb the sight of the packed room. He felt a wave of awe at the sheer number of people who had gathered.

"Wow," he said, his voice filled with emotion. "I wish El could see this." Though deep down, he was certain El was present. "I know this room is just a fraction of the students El mentored. Thank you all for being here."

Rick took a deep breath, steadying himself, and explained how El had outlined the celebration. There would be no assigned speakers, no long eulogies. Instead, the gathering was limited to thirty minutes, after which music would play, and everyone would be free to mingle and reminisce. El had only one request — that they enjoy themselves. "This is a celebration," Rick added, "and El would want us to treat it that way."

With the formalities addressed, Rick said, "I guess I'll start." He hesitated for a moment, gathering his thoughts, hoping his brief words could somehow encompass the countless lessons his mentor had taught him.

"It feels too cliché to say we're here to pay respects to a man we all know and love. While that's true, I believe we're also here to pay tribute to the artistry of his life. El didn't just live — he created. There was an artistry in the way he viewed the world, the way he taught, and the way he lived."

Rick paused, his throat tightening with emotion. He cleared his throat and continued.

"Lines are a simple thing
Lines are what we make them
Drawn wrong, and they'll make you sad
Drawn right, and they'll make you glad
Lines have the power to transform nothing into something
Lines on a blank page can create a masterpiece
You can lay down the line
You can pick up the line
Stand in line and complain, or
Stand in line to experience the ride of your life
We can walk a crooked line, or
We can walk a straight and narrow path
A fallen power line can electrocute
A power line can light the world
Lovers can cross the line
While others wait for their lines to cross
Lines can box us in, or
You can break through the lines to start anew
A few sharp lines can destroy a heart
A few smooth lines can spark a love
Railroad lines were used by enemies to deliver death
Railroad lines have been used for years to deliver food to the
hungry, clothing to the naked
People form picket lines to show their anger and frustration
People form lines to pay respect and express their love
Lines can signal the end of an addiction
Lines can signal the start of something new
Lines are what we make them, they are in our control
They can be a lifeline or a noose
Each line waits for us to choose
After all, lines are a powerful thing
They can turn nothing into something"

As Rick closed, he let his gaze sweep over the crowd, tender yet purposeful. "El would remind us — design your life well. Begin your work now, while there's still ink to be drawn. This is your canvas, and only you hold the pen. Live intentionally. No excuses."

As his words lingered in the air, an almost sacred silence enveloped the room. Then, as if orchestrated by unseen hands, every line in the building — the painted murals, the intricate carvings, the sketches on display — began to emit a soft, ethereal blue glow. The light pulsed faintly at first, then intensified, illuminating the studio in an otherworldly brilliance. The energy was tangible, humming through the air like a heartbeat shared among all present. It wasn't just light; it was connection — a vibrant thread tying everyone together, weaving them into El's legacy and the intricate lines of their own lives.

Rick stood frozen, the electric glow reflected in his wide eyes. The moment transcended explanation, as though the studio itself had come alive, responding to the collective emotion that filled its walls. It was a final, breathtaking gift from El — a reminder of the infinite power contained in a single line and the limitless possibilities it could inspire.

Breaking the stillness, Rick's voice softened, yet it carried a concrete message as he looked into the eyes of those gathered. "So now, I ask you — how will you align your life?"

BE THE LINE MAKER

This moment isn't random — it's kairos.

This blank canvas is yours. Pick up your pen. Make your mark.

What's one lesson from this book you can apply right now?

Live Intentionally. No Excuses.

Take a pic of the line you've drawn and share it to
Be the Line Maker on LinkedIn, Instagram, or Facebook.

ABOUT THE AUTHOR

Brett Armstrong is a storyteller, speaker, and creative leader whose work explores the art of intentional living and leadership. Through *The Line Maker,* he invites readers to rediscover creativity, purpose, and the courage to make their mark.

Blending insights from leadership, human behavior, and the creative process, Brett helps people navigate change with intention — and design lives worthy of becoming their greatest masterpiece. As a creative strategist, he has helped lead disruptive organizations and underperforming teams to success by finding talent, developing leaders, and transforming potential into performance — even in the most unlikely places.

Whether on the golf course, crafting marketing copy, or writing song lyrics now streaming on Spotify, Brett continues to discover the power of a single line — one that can connect, inspire, and transform nothing into something grand. Yet his favorite masterpiece is the one he's creating at home with his family — where love, laughter, and legacy intersect.

BOOK BRETT ARMSTRONG
TO SPEAK WITH YOUR TEAM, CONFERENCE, OR ORGANIZATION

Brett Armstrong delivers transformative keynotes inspired by *The Line Maker*.

Through powerful storytelling and practical strategy, he helps individuals and teams reimagine how they live, lead, and act with intention.

His keynotes challenge audiences to:

- Step up to the line when the pressure is on

- Turn disruption into direction

- Understand what's really happening during uncomfortable times of change

- Align communication, accountability, and purpose

- Lead with creativity, courage, and conviction

- **Build a legacy that outlives your timeline — one intentional line at a time**

LIVE (AND LEAD) INTENTIONALLY. NO EXCUSES.

 TheLineMaker   BeTheLineMaker   BeTheLineMaker

Brett is represented by **The Gray+Miller Agency**, a leading bureau representing the world's most engaging thought leaders.

For speaking inquiries visit graymilleragency.com or connect at BeTheLineMaker.com

PUT *THE LINE MAKER* INTO ACTION

Now that you've decided to draw the line and make your mark, it's time to live it.

The **DESIGN Framework** is your next step toward intentional living — a simple six-step guide to help you align your lines, act with purpose, and create progress that lasts.

When you register, you'll receive:

- **A digital guide** on how to apply *The Line Maker* principles and design your legacy

- **Regular insights and prompts** to help you live, learn, love, and lead with intention

- **Access to future live sessions** and exclusive resources

SCAN THE QR CODE TO GET STARTED AND DOWNLOAD YOUR FREE GUIDE:
"Make Your Mark: The Line Maker's Guide to Design"

Or visit www.BeTheLineMaker.com

HAVE A TEAM?

Brett loves working with organizations to elevate leadership and culture.

Contact him to explore **team sessions, culture workshops, and new leadership development experiences** built on *The Line Maker* principles.

Representing a community of authors whose books have collectively sold hundreds of millions of copies, the founders of The Gray + Miller Agency launched Maison Vero, a professional publishing house that partners with rising authors to bring their thought leadership to the world. Our representation covers every aspect of thought leadership, including U.S. senators, governors, and ambassadors, billionaire founders and entrepreneurs, researchers, academics, scientists, consultants, practitioners, social influencers, C-suite leaders, adventurers, professional athletes, artists, and creators. We partner with thought leaders and world changers like you who have a story to tell. By bringing decades of professional expertise to our clients, we are charting a new path in a timeless industry that transcends publishing norms, transforming powerful thoughts into impactful books that inspire minds, ignite hearts, and open doors.

Visit maisonvero.com to view our growing list of authors, or to submit a proposal for publication consideration.

Follow Maison Vero for insight and inspiration on social media:

 MaisonVero    MaisonVero   MaisonVeroPublishing

For information about special discounts for bulk purchases, please call 1-949-333-4872 or email info@graymilleragency.com.

Maison Vero is a partner brand of The Gray + Miller Agency, a speaking, literary, and talent consortium. For more information on the talent represented by The Gray + Miller Agency, or to bring any of our thought leaders to your organization or live event, please visit our website at graymilleragency.com.